ATTACK OF THE TODDLERS!

FURTHER ADVENTURES ON PLANET PARENTHOOD

Julie Tilsner

Contemporary Books

Chicago   New York   San Francisco   Lisbon   London   Madrid   Mexico City
Milan   New Delhi   San Juan   Seoul   Singapore   Sydney   Toronto

Library of Congress Cataloging-in-Publication Data

Tilsner, Julie.
  Attack of the toddlers! : further adventures on Planet Parenthood /
Julie Tilsner.
    p.   cm.
  ISBN 0-8092-9749-3
  1. Toddlers.   2. Parenting.   3. Child rearing.   I. Title.
HQ774.5.T55   2001
649'.12—dc21

2001017360

Contemporary Books

A Division of The ***McGraw-Hill*** *Companies*

1 2 3 4 5 6 7 8 9 0   AGM/AGM   0 9 8 7 6 5 4 3 2 1

ISBN: 0-8092-9749-3

This book was set in Minion by Susan H. Hartman
Printed and bound by Quebecor—Martinsburg

Cover illustration copyright © David McMacken

McGraw-Hill books are available at special quantity discounts to use as premiums and sales promotions, or for use in corporate training programs. For more information, please write to the Director of Special Sales, Professional Publishing, McGraw-Hill, Two Penn Plaza, New York, NY 10121-2298. Or contact your local bookstore.

This book is printed on acid-free paper.

CONTENTS

1   Them   1
Toddlers—Who They Are, What They Want

Portrait of a One-Year-Old • Identifying Toddlers: A Field Guide • What Do They Want? • Enter the Sun King and His Courtiers (That's You) • Know the Beast • Obsession • The Difference Between Babies and Toddlers • Picking Your Battles • The Four-Way Path • Translation Nation

2   Slave Parents from Beyond Infinity   39

Grinding Routine • Spelling Skills • Objects of Compulsion • Toddler Support Group • Play Date Etiquette • Tapping Your Inner Toddler • It's a Toddler Thing • In the House of the Rising Tot • Becoming the

PREFACE

By the end of Year One, you're a hardened parent.
You don't scare easily anymore. And good thing, too.
Because at this point, your baby is starting to seem, well, less like
a baby and more like an actual person. She's walking
or making ready to walk. She can point to whatever she's interested
in. She might be saying a few words. Her likes and
dislikes are very clear. Her personality is fully formed, and she's a
master at getting you to do her every bidding. From here it's
one big slippery slope into toddlerhood, which is a
completely different parenting enchilada. You're going to need
all your newfound skills to navigate the next twelve months.
Good luck.
—from Planet Parenthood:
Adapting to Your New Life-Form

Annie became a toddler one day a few months after her first birthday. After weeks of chuckling over what at the time was a new phenomenon, the Teletubbies, my husband, Luke, and I decided to bring a tape of the show home to show her, more as a social experiment than anything. If nothing else, we were curious to see what all the fuss was about.

Our first thought, upon seeing the bright colors, the rabbits, the talking flowers, and that little baby boy in the sun, was "Whoa! Psychedelic, man!" Had we been ten years younger (or our own ages, but not parents), this would have made a killer party video. It was a trip. And while Luke and I sat there tripping, our fifteen-month-old daughter got hooked.

She screamed. She danced. She laughed and pointed. And when finally the little happy boy in the sun went down at the end of the show, Annie waved bye-bye, then threw herself to the floor and wept.

We had to watch that wretched tape five times in a row. And that was just the first night. When we tried to redirect her attention to something more productive and stimulating—say, for example, dinner—she sobbed and kicked her feet in a manner we'd never seen before. I related all these symptoms to my mother, hoping for an explanation. She had one, of course.

"Annie's turned into a toddler," she said, and started laughing.

Toddlers, like obscenity, are hard to define. But, with the help of this book, you'll definitely know them when you see them. Moreover, you'll be able to speak their language, sidestep many major battles, get some nutritious food into them, and even, God willing, enjoy them for what they are. Indeed, after you've lived through your child's toddler years, you'll be able to handle almost anything this world can throw at you, including the teenage years.

What's that U.S. Army jingle? It's the hardest job you'll ever love? Parenting a toddler is kind of like that.

I see a lot of toddlers. Because my husband is currently a graduate student, we live in a student family housing complex that is cheap, small, dowdy, and crawling with small children. We love it. One of our many neighbors described the place perfectly: "It's like a twenty-four-hour child observation laboratory." So true.

In the course of writing this book, I've seen toddlers when they're fresh-cheeked angels singing at the top of their lungs just because they're happy, and I've seen toddlers when they've turned into screaming, thrashing beasts because another toddler looked at them too long. I've witnessed the panicked look on a parent's face when their young toddler starts running around the courtyard screaming "No! No! No!" to no one in particular. I've held several "Toddler Summits" with my neighbors to try and tap into the unique frame of mind and special skills necessary to survive toddlerhood. It's been rich fodder, and it ultimately led me to title this book *Attack of the Toddlers!*, because at the end of the day, that's the only verb a parent can pull up to describe the exhausting, exasperating, and hilarious antics of their tots in the last twenty-four hours.

But I can see you want a bit more in the way of example, don't you? Fair enough.

As I write this, my neighbor Emily is doing battle downstairs with her two-and-a-half-year-old daughter Magda. Emily has just come home from work (she's a post-doc, which is to say, she's got a Ph.D. and teaches classes to undergraduates but isn't a professor yet—it's a form of slave labor unique to academia). In between work and picking up her daughter from day care, she had a fit of ambition and went grocery shopping as well. Now her daughter, who didn't take a nap today, is refusing to get out of the car seat.

If you've got a toddler, you already know where this is headed.

Anyway, with her husband still at work, Emily's on her own with this one. She tries verbally goading Magda out of the car as she schlepps the grocery bags one by one to the foot of the stairs. Nothing works, until finally she lies and tells Magda that my daughter Annie is in the courtyard waiting to play with her. Whoops. This is a tactical error.

Magda leaps from the car and races into the courtyard, which gets Emily that much closer to herding her upstairs, where she can change her diaper, feed her, and get her down for an hour for a much-needed nap. But Magda soon realizes that Annie isn't, in fact, in the courtyard, and that she's been had.

Toddlers hate to be had.

Emily, a grocery bag in either hand, tries to act nonchalant. "C'mon honey. Let's go upstairs."

Magda glowers at her and doesn't move.

They stare at each other. The sizing up begins. Emily tries her Mom voice.

"I mean it now. I've got to change you. Let's go. Right now."

Magda sets her lip. Here it comes.

"No."

The staredown continues. Emily puts her bags down.

"Magda, come here."

"No!" Magda stomps her foot. The particular pitch to that declarative leads me to believe she's digging in for the long haul.

"Magda . . ."

The girl makes a break for it. "Noooooo!" She runs deep into the courtyard as the milk in the grocery bags starts to sour and the ice cream starts to melt.

Emily looks up at me as if seeking an explanation for all of this.

"She's two and a half," I shrug.

At one of our many toddler summits, we, the parents of toddlers, would look at this scenario and agree that the only way Emily will get her daughter upstairs is if she employs one of three time-honored toddler wrangling methods:

1. Bribery (video, candy, juice, Daddy)

2. Distraction (somehow get her to forget the present battle; then revisit it again in ten minutes when she might be more amenable to coming upstairs)

3. Brute strength (pick the damn kid up and bring her upstairs)

The groceries will have to wait until the toddler is placated in some way. (I always put the perishables away first and forget the rest for someone else to put away.) But another screaming match is almost certain to ensue in almost any case, because a tired, hungry adult is no match for a tired, hungry toddler.

Sound familiar? It will. This is your world for the next several years. The toddler years are indeed an attack: an attack on your physical and mental well-being. An attack on your love of order and rationality. An attack on your original hair color. You'll emerge out the other end with a four-year-old who may or may not have calmed down into a more pliant being, but at least you'll be better than a weatherman at seeing the tantrum coming down the pike, and you'll do whatever is necessary to nip it in the bud.

Annie is now almost four, which means she's really moved out of the toddler realm and into the preschool set. She still has her moments, usually when she's hungry or tired, when she wants to supersede the laws of physics and get her spaghetti now versus waiting for it to cook. But because we've lived through the Attack, we know how to talk her down from most impending tantrums, or at least herd her into a safe room if we can't. We don't hesitate to use bribery or tough negotiation when the situation merits. And although she can still prolong her bedtime routine until 10 P.M., she at least will agree to sit quietly in bed looking at books until she falls asleep.

At almost four, she's starting to resemble us.

Luke and I, however, have become a lot more toddler-like in the process. This happens to everyone who's ever raised a toddler. It will happen to you, too.

The other day a neighbor and her two-year-old son dropped by to say hi. Luke and I were letting Annie watch an episode of "Blue's Clues," but as usual we were soon sitting on the floor watching it, too.

The little boy ran back into Annie's room, and before long the two of them were playing with her plastic kitchenette. Meanwhile, we three adults sat in the living room, glued to the set. We didn't budge until the end of the episode.

"That was a good one," remarked my neighbor. "I hadn't seen it before."

"Yeah," I said. "It's a new one. Just came out."

"I'll have to run out and get Amir a copy," she said.

"Yeah. He'll love it," I said. "Especially the dancing crab part."

"Yeah."

We sat silently as the next episode began. The kids stayed in the bedroom, from the sounds of it, "drinking" coffee. The opening credits were just about over when Luke spoke up.

"We're watching 'Blue's Clues' and we're enjoying it. What's happened to us?"

"Shhh!" I hissed. "Steve's about to sing."

ACKNOWLEDGMENTS

This book couldn't have happened without the good folks in the courtyard, University Village, University of California, Berkeley. They are, in no particular order: Julia Regalado and Javier Alvarez-Mon, Jane and Luis Huerta, Mindy Swanson and Peter Brownell, Stafford Gregoire and Linda Chandler, Misti Hassan, Laura Fontan-Dixon, Eric and Cheri Schultzke, Emily Gottreich, Watiri Boylen, and Shams and Inji Tantawy.

And, of course, the toddlers: Lulu, Claudia, Nicola, Chandler, Mason, Amir, Clifford, Magda, Lydia, Vera, Don Yeoung, Daniel, Christine, Andrew, and Yusef.

Special thanks to my editor, Matthew Carnicelli, for his steadfast patience and constant good humor.

INTRODUCTION

Dawn of the Mutant Babies

I wouldn't be so smug if I were you.

Sure, you've survived one full year with a baby in your house. Sure, the little fellow is awfully cute these days. He's crawling, maybe even walking, all over the place, pointing out the wonders of the world and looking up at you brimming with adoration of your superior powers. He's just the cutest thing in the world, and darn near everyone who gets near him thinks so, too. (They're not just saying that!) As for yourselves, you're feeling pretty proud. Look at that perfect child, you beam. We raised him ourselves. We've successfully mastered parenting.

But I wouldn't let your guard down just yet. Changes are afoot that are going to change your life again. Maybe not on the magnitude introducing a baby into your duo did, but a devastating rift just the same.

Yes, I know you've heard of the Terrible Twos, and you're thinking you've got another whole year to bask in your baby's compliancy. Take it from me, you've got another few months, maybe not even that, depending on the personality of your baby, before the poop hits the fan.

For the baby, toddlerhood is a lurch into personhood. In the first year their job was to stay alive and grow to a certain size and learn certain skills that would enable them to do humanlike tasks such as walking and picking Cheerios out of a cup. These next couple of years takes this basic model and adds personality, ego, awareness, and determination, along with a bad attitude. It means that suddenly, your happy little baby has clued into what you're having, and he wants some, too, damn it.

Sure, you're bigger and stronger, but heft and brawn are not enough to win the Attack of the Toddlers. A toddler has more energy than you. He's more ambitious and more frustrated. Moreover, he's not bound by any of the social restraints or notions of decorum that you are. Heck, even the laws of physics mean nothing to him. He doesn't know what he wants half of the time, but when he does, he wants what he wants and he wants it now—and who are you to try and stop him?

Unfortunately, you're the parent.

It falls to you to capture and civilize this person. Not only to keep him safe and warm, but to teach him why it's not OK to bite other people and why words work better than screaming and why he should eat his scrambled eggs even if they look different than they did yesterday.

You'll find that the next two years will be a constantly shifting battle of wits. From about fifteen months through the end of the third year, your toddler will grow more and more adept at thwarting your attempts to civilize her. Dogs and monkeys can be trained to perform certain tricks, and it's true that a toddler can learn how to, say, brush her teeth each night. But the trouble with a toddler is that, unlike a lesser primate, she is able to analyze the nightly schedule and find your weak spots and thus create a hundred different ways to avoid having to brush her teeth until it personally benefits her. Toddlers are cute but masterful manipulators. They should be running the United Nations instead of the grownups.

They're physically a lot more advanced than babies as well, obviously. From the time you begin playing the Stay in the Car Seat game, you'll long for the days when your infant went where you went and never complained.

A toddler is mobile. He can get wherever he wants of his own free will, except when one of his parents foil him. This happens a great deal, since young toddlers have all the dexterity but none of the sense to keep themselves out of danger. The middle of the street and the swimming pool appeal to them equally. Ditto that pot of water on the stove or the neighbors' crotchety old cat. Toddlers learn how to open the front door lock and head for the park before you even get out of the bathroom, and by the time they're three, they know exactly when you usually go into the bathroom and for how long.

The simple methods of childproofing you used when she was a baby just don't cut it anymore, either. Sure, those cookies were safe in the cabinet above the counter just a few months ago. But that was before she learned the principles of stacking and of elevation. Now she simply pushes the chair over to the counter, stands on the chair, climbs onto the counter, opens the cupboard, and voilà! Cookie smorgasbord. It's a developmental milestone that you would be celebrating, if it didn't significantly complicate your life.

Cupboard locks, you say? They're child's play for your average toddler. My neighbor Laura tells me her two-year-old son, Cliff, already knows how to circumvent the safety latch on the dryer and is well on his way to figuring out how to dismantle the entire machine.

Toddlers develop new skills and awareness of what's going on around them so quickly you will always underestimate them. As such, it's up to you, oh hapless parent, to keep a constant and wary eye on your tot, so that you can correctly determine where they are today on the IQ scale and adopt more sophisticated methods of trickery. It's an elaborate dance of intrigue, the toddler years. I'm surprised Hollywood hasn't done anything with the concept.

The textbook rationale behind toddlers is that they're in that tough transition between babies and little people. You can blame all the tantrums and mood swings on their frustrations of wanting to be more independent, but not being so. They're alarmingly like teenagers in that respect, I'm told. Great.

But it makes sense, I suppose, that the root of all the drama lies with their growing pains. If we were growing more aware of our surroundings and making connections between a million different things, we'd probably be cranky, too. Ignorance, as they say, is bliss.

Keep that in mind as you pick your way through the toddler minefield.

As I've said before, I have no credentials other than being a mom myself. No fancy acronyms following my name. No time spent at medical school. I do, however, live at ground zero, toddler country. Every day I get to watch toddlers in their native environment. I hear their screams, watch them try to share, listen to their parents try to reason with them, and, in more cases than not, watch as they pick up their rampaging toddlers and bring them inside for a time-out.

The Toddler Summit Manifesto

We, the Parents of Toddlers worldwide, declare that in order to preserve sanity and some semblance of household order, the following toddler truisms must be embraced:

- Rational argument is impossible.
- "Because I said so, and I'm the mommy/daddy" is a perfectly valid argument.
- Sanity, thy name is VCR.
- Sharing is an ideal to work toward.
- Bribery is good.
- The five basic food groups are open to wide interpretation.
- Pick your battles (and choose wisely).

Attack of the Toddlers! is a field guide to identifying and surviving the unique beast that is a toddler. I've culled through my own experiences, etched as they are into my memory like so many teeth marks, and tapped into the collective wisdom of the Toddler Summit to give you, oh perplexed parent, the benefit of experience. If you want a serious book on the developmental reasons behind this age group, or if you're one of those cheerful, can-do types who chafe at the very phrase "terrible twos," you probably want a different book. If you haven't yet gone through the toddler years but think you'll be able to do it without ever screaming at, bribing, or physically restraining your child, I doff my hat and respectfully suggest that you need this book more than anyone.

I hope at the very least to impart the wisdom that no matter how crazy the next few years are, you're not in it alone. There is always someone out there who can top your toddler horror story.

We start by taking an in-depth look at "Them"—because you can't survive the toddler years if you don't know what you're up against. In Chapter 1 you'll learn how to identify toddlers in the wild, distinct traits you'll want to know about, and how best to handle the toddler attack. For those of you who aren't sure what you have in the crib, we examine exactly what makes a toddler distinct from a baby. Once we've learned all about them, we can learn all about you in the next chapter, "Slave Parents from Beyond Infinity." It's true that when your child was still a baby, he so charmed you you'd do anything for him. Well now that he's a toddler, he's perfected his methods of dominating you. Sure, you think you're the boss, but in reality, he is. And let's face it, you'll do just about anything to prevent him from screaming, won't you? We'll meet other toddler parents and learn why they're so important to your mental health.

"The Taming of the Beast" describes all the necessary rules for taming your toddler and turning him into a productive, nonscreaming member of society, including the task parents dread most, potty training. We examine why consistency and discipline start to play a starring role in your attempt at being a good parent, as well as all the household routines it's now time to acclimatize your little beast to.

Following the civilization theme, "Tales from Day Care" takes it a bit further and looks at what happens once you introduce your toddler to the wider world out there. What happens, you ask? Pokémon happens. Disney happens. Tantrums, of course, have happened all along, only now they happen in public, and you need to know how to keep a straight face while waiting them out.

Like most parents, you may think you're out of the dark, scary, toddler woods once your child turns three. But you're all wrong, oh, so terribly wrong. The older toddler is a more agile, more determined, crankier version of himself at two. In short, he's at the top of his game. "I Spit on Your Tricycle" is all about the advanced toddler wrangling skills you'll need when dealing with this creature known as a three-year-old. How to identify her when she's being a puppy or a shark. How to manage her whining and get her to request something other than cookies for every meal. We'll shed light on various enrichment fantasies and why no Sunday afternoon will ever turn out how you planned now that you have a toddler in tow.

Welcome to Year Two and beyond on Planet Parenthood. I didn't want to mention this last year, because you certainly didn't need anything more to worry about. But peer out onto the horizon for a moment.

See them?

They're toddlers. And they're coming this way.

THEM

Toddlers— Who They Are, What They Want

Q: What's the difference between terrorists and toddlers?

A: You can negotiate with terrorists.

In the first year of your new lives as parents, you tended to focus on the obvious: your baby's physical and mental growth. There are all those milestones to meet: first smile by six weeks, first tooth by three months, first food at six months, crawling by eight, pulling up by ten, and, of course, the Big Kahoona of milestones—walking—anytime between nine and fifteen months.

It was a tiring year, you betcha. And that big, expensive first-year birthday party you threw was, face it, really more for you, celebrating the fact that you got through the inaugural year of parenthood. No doubt you feel justified in taking the next twelve months off, a sort of vacation time between the first birthday and the start of the infamous Terrible Twos. I'm so sorry to have to tell you this, but there ain't no vacation time granted on Planet Parenthood. Once your baby has demonstrated that he'd rather walk than eat, your time is nigh. You're staring into the face of toddlerhood, and your parenting experience is going to radically downshift into a throatier, more physical realm.

There are many who would say that parenting, in the verb form, doesn't come into play until the toddler years. I'd have to agree with that. Lots of parents catch on to the daily care and feeding of an infant but completely fall apart when faced with a small child who starts to violently scream when asked to put the Play-Doh away.

Parenting a toddler isn't for the weak of heart, flabby of muscle, or undecided of mind. It takes a will like a steel trap, to mix clichés, to maintain a consistent, united front for the next few years. But you must, because it gets a lot harder before it gets easier. While a young toddler is merely a walking destructive force, an older toddler has mapped out a number of very mercenary ways to get what he wants, and it's up to you to force moderation upon him. A hundred times a day your parenting boils down to this: it's you against him. The mother of all battle of wills.

I know, I know. It sounds like this parenting-a-toddler gig should only be attempted by professionals. If we had to assemble a dream team for the job, a partial roster might include

- Madeline Albright—To negotiate with irrational despots and maniacal warlords.

- Michael Jordan—To chase, catch, and force opponent to do your bidding. Strong knees for endless games of Tiger/Horsey/Dinosaur.

- Martha Stewart—To devise clever games and toys out of common household items such as tinfoil and string. To make food that resembles small barnyard animals.

- The Dalai Lama—To keep a serene demeanor in the face of chaos. By which we mean a Force Three tantrum in a crowded parking lot with an armful of groceries because you didn't let your two-year-old hold the car keys. *Ooooooommmmmm.*

Think you're up to the job? Didn't think so. I wasn't, either, but I've almost made it through the toddler years. And if I can do it, anyone can. So what if I have to see my hair colorist every six weeks?

Portrait of a One-Year-Old

Your twelve-monther is on the brink of a great adventure. Not quite a toddler, she's nevertheless regarding the world around her with a gleam in her eye. She's just learned how to walk or is just about to, and suddenly her universe is larger than it's ever been. More tantalizing, too. She's got enough social development to know which adult is most likely to get her what she wants, although it will be another two years before she's polished this particular skill to a killing gloss. She's starting to develop her own, very particular tastes about what she puts in her mouth, who holds her and when, and whether or not she wants to let you put her shoes on. She's still enough of a baby to need you for almost everything, but in the months to come, her thinking on that is going to change dramatically, even if yours doesn't. If you listen closely enough, you can hear the drums of toddlerhood in the distance. And they're getting louder. . . .

Identifying Toddlers: A Field Guide

Toddlers occur the world over. When you're shaking your head over why your eighteen-month-old won't eat any green food any more, rest assured that across the world, another toddler, same age, is doing the same thing in China, only she's decided to boycott rice. Even though you probably don't speak each other's languages, you and the Chinese parents would understand each other completely. It's the universal language of perplexity.

Any discussion of toddlerhood, however, should start with a working definition of *toddler*. It's a cute word, of unknown coinage, invoking all sorts of adorable diaper commercials and Hallmark cards in which a perfect little baby, backlit, of course, and wearing a diaphanous gown, suddenly stands up and tromps from foot to foot toward the outstretched hands of his beaming parents. Technically, I suppose, this is what *toddler* means: a baby who develops the bravado to walk and proceeds to toddle from foot to foot. What the Hallmark commercials never show you, of course, is the path of destruction they leave in their wake.

Ah, but *when* does a toddler become a *toddler*? This is open to wide interpretation. Doctors will say it's a developmental thing, involving not only toddling but a growing general mastery of things physical, including jumping and running and talking and the desire to wallop others of their ilk. Psychologists will talk about the emergence of ego, of self, of a drive toward separation from mother and toward greater independence. Me? I say toddlerhood is a state of mind.

Toddler Time Line

Early (15 to 18 months)—Mobility plus attitude equals toddlerhood.

Early Middle (18 months to 2 years)—There's just no reasoning with some people—like everyone in this toddler bracket.

Classic Period (2 to 2½ years)—No to everything.

Late Toddlerhood (2½ to 3 years)—It's life, but not as you remember it.

Surprise Attack (3 to 4 years)—It ain't over till the fat lady is almost in kindergarten.

Your thirteen-month-old may indeed be tottering from room to room. But if she's still letting you strap her into her car seat, she ain't a toddler yet.

It Begins . . .

The day will come when you look down at the fruit of your loins and realize that your sweet little pliant baby has mutated into a toddler avenger. Trouble is, toddlerhood is a surprise attack: it's not for you to know when this will happen. And every baby seems to turn at a different date.

Meg and Doug's daughter Molly, for example, was barely thirteen months when she refused to get into her parents' rental car. It was red, you see. Not the color of the car she was used to. "It took both of us—using full strength—to get her into the car seat," recalls Meg. "It just came out of the

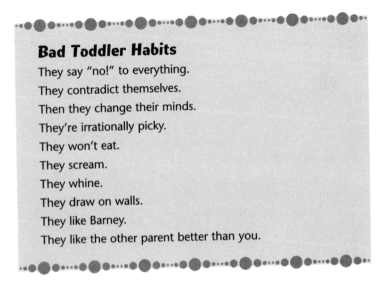

Bad Toddler Habits
They say "no!" to everything.
They contradict themselves.
Then they change their minds.
They're irrationally picky.
They won't eat.
They scream.
They whine.
They draw on walls.
They like Barney.
They like the other parent better than you.

blue. One day she decided to fight us tooth and nail over *everything*."

My friend Mimi's son merely gave her the hairy eyeball.

"I asked him to please come to Mommy, and he turned around and gave me this look I'd never seen before," she recalls. "Then he turned and ran away."

Balkiness. Running away. Yep. It's all there on the check-list. The exact age when these qualities start to grow in your child, however, isn't. That's why you have to remain vigilant and keep your guard way up, especially after baby has learned to walk. Upward mobility is really just one big slippery slope into toddlerhood. But there are other signs you should be watching for.

Sure Signs of Impending Toddlerhood
You don't need a compass to know which way the wind is blowing . . .

- Screaming replaces cooing, pointing, and other forms of communication.

- Runs away from you at every opportunity.

- Sudden refusal to be put into car seat, stroller, or backpack.

- Extreme contrariness.

- Strange new obsessions.

- Sudden realization of the existence of baked goods and confectionery.

- Refusal of all previously eaten food (except for previously mentioned baked goods and confectionery).

- Selective hearing.

Julia's daughter Lulu just turned one recently, but already the signs are there. She points at objects in front of her that nobody else can see, gets every adult in the room picking up everything in sight and asking, "This? What? This?" and then starts to cry as if insulted by our collective idiocy. If her mother tries to give her a spoonful of the wrong morsel, she pushes her mother's hand away until she gets what she wants. She screams in frustration when her attempts to sit in puddles are foiled. And, of course, when her mother calls her, she runs the other way. Julia just shakes her head. "I didn't think it would start this early," she tells me. I shrug and grimace. I've got a three-and-a-half-year-old.

"It's gonna get a lot worse before it gets better," I say. It sounds like an apology.

A lot of times a baby turns into a toddler almost overnight. One day you'll put your baby down for her nap, and when she wakes up, she's a toddler. One minute she's an easily pleased, mellow baby, the next, she's a surly, opinionated, pushy stranger, as if she went to bed a Californian and woke up a New Yorker. Most parents will tell you that their toddler has an altogether different personality than their baby, and they've had to learn how to deal with issues they never saw coming: a proclivity toward biting, for example. Or an extreme aversion to Uncle Bob. "She turns two, and suddenly she's grabby and nasty," says my neighbor of her recently two-year-old daughter, Vera. "All she says to anybody anymore is 'No!'" I know another woman whose angelic, even-tempered little boy seemed to morph in the space of one week into an aggressive little monster who screamed in response to every challenge and became the bane of his play group. The other moms secretly began referring to him as Fang Boy. All his poor mother could do was try to soothe the wailing children he bit and placate their moms. Even she didn't know what happened. "Where did my baby go?" she'd moan.

A dramatic change like this can shock you and throw you off your parenting game for months. Take my advice and don't spend too long wondering what happened—your toddler is evolving already, and he's learning your weaknesses even as you wander the house with your head in your hands. You've got to adapt to this new creature and deal with him. Or else.

What Do They Want?

A toddler has several basic goals in life. The first seems to be the desire to test you to your limits. Even though he may well know that he's not supposed to play with the electrical socket (because you've been firmly telling him not to ever since he could first crawl up to it), a bona fide toddler will look you in the eye and proceed to finger said socket, just to see what you'll do. Then he'll do it again, just to make sure. Then he'll try it when you're not looking. Then he'll sneak out of bed to try it, and so on, and so on. Indeed, as he grows from an early toddler to a late toddler, his methods of testing you become ever more bold and diabolical, until you're ready to keep him chained to a post in his bedroom, at which time he'll turn four years old and become a pliant, ready-to-please wonder child.

Toddlers and Teens: A Connection?

Wiser folks than us have commented on the eerie similarities between teenagers and toddlers. From my standpoint, the biggest difference is that teenagers are tall enough to climb out of windows and know how to light cigarettes, not that a toddler couldn't do either of these things if he really put his mind to it.

If nothing else, it might be helpful to think of the toddler years as practice for the teenage years to come. Here are some alarming similarities between toddlers and teenagers that should serve to remind you that even after your child stops watching "Sesame Street," you aren't out of the woods yet.

- **Surliness**—Don't talk to me. Don't look at me. Leave me alone. Don't tell me what to do. Sound familiar?
- **Odd fashion sense**—All toddlers go through a period of insisting that they pick out their own clothes. Worse, they also insist on putting on these clothes themselves. Not only then are you dealing with, say, a green bathing suit over purple and blue striped pants, but the pants are probably on backward and the bathing suit is inside

Why is this? The experts say it's because along with a greater mobility comes an increased desire for independence, and that means figuring out what he can get away with on his own. Of course, at the same time your toddler wants to go off and explore his new horizons, he also wants you there right behind him telling him what to do. If this sounds irrational and confusing, think how the toddler must feel.

out. Don't think for a minute that you'll be able to convince your tot to change before venturing out into public, because the more you protest the more insistent she'll become, and she may just add an umbrella to the ensemble as well. A teenager will probably concoct getups that are somewhat more *considered,* but rest assured, it will vex you just as much. Indeed, the blasé attitude you cultivated and hopefully perfected with your toddler will go far in your favor now.

- **Food pickiness**—Your toddler may eat only white rice and mashed potatoes while you knock yourself out fixing her more nutritious fare. Hopefully, you won't even bother trying to get your adolescent to eat more than Diet Peach Snapple and Doritos chips.
- **Sneakiness**—Many toddlers do what they know darn well they're not supposed to do, when they think you're not looking. You no doubt remember the kind of antics you got up to as a teenager, don't you? I do, anyway. And the only difference I can see is that toddlers steal cookies instead of Mom's expensive scotch.

Enter the Sun King and His Courtiers (That's You)

Another of a toddler's basic goals is immediate gratification at all costs. During the early toddler years, a child isn't aware that anyone exists but himself. To his way of thinking, the universe *does* revolve around him. By the time he's out of his threes, your tot allegedly does understand that there are others to consider besides himself, but he's still very skilled at ignoring this fact.

Since your job is to thwart 75 percent of what the toddler wants to do, eat, or rub in his hair, denial of immediate gratification constitutes the cause of most of the problems you'll be experiencing between now and sometime after the third year.

And your toddler will not be amused. Scary as it sounds, it's not really stretching things to compare your toddler to Louis XIV or a similar despot.

You'll notice I said "despot." I did not say "enlightened."

If you can't dig on a despot (or you don't want to look the term up), think of a toddler as a rock diva, or a Fortune 500 chief executive. Or the shoe-in presidential candidate. Gone forever are the days when your happy baby complied with all you asked of him. Now it's all about ego and immediate gratification and things done his way or not at all. You'll have to start thinking of yourself as the handler/manager of this person. You know his needs better than anyone else, and you guide his career along to the best of your ability. You try to avoid the issues you know will set him off, but when the tantrums do come, you take them in stride. (You'll learn this skill later, trust me.)

When the Sun King arrives, you'll have to make certain concessions. The Sun King has his own ideas about everything: when he rises in the morning and what he will wear today. He's decided that he will only have the Cheerios for breakfast and only in the Mickey Mouse bowl. There will be one-half cup of orange juice, not apple, not grape, placed to the right of his bowl. Too high to the right may set him off or not, depending on his overall mood.

I don't want to infer that you're soon to become an indentured servant to the king. Think more along the lines of some cranky but influential cardinal, the power behind the throne.

Your toddler understands this; it's just that he chooses to ignore it. He's compelled by nature to push the outer limits and see how far you'll let him go. He really can't help himself. The books all promise that even while he's fighting you tooth and claw as you tie him down into the car seat, he really does feel more secure knowing he can't take advantage of you. Try to remember this as you treat your wounds later on. There's probably something to it.

Know the Beast

In war, as in parenthood, it helps to know what you're up against. How can you tell a toddler from, say, a preschooler? Here are some telltale signs.

Grimy Face

Before I had my own, I swore that when I had kids I would never let them run around with runny noses and smudgy faces. My children, I swore, would always have clean, pink faces and pristine hands. Then, when my daughter reached a certain age, I quickly learned that it is impossible to keep a roaming tot free of schmutz, and I stopped trying. Why is it impossible? Law of nature, apparently. Filthy is their natural state.

Constant Motion

Toddlers have two speeds: on and off. If they're off, they're sound asleep on the floor, in your lap, under the table, or anywhere it's most inconvenient for you. If they're on, well, you're on, too. Babies are known for sometimes sitting back in their bouncy chairs and taking it all in. Toddlers don't do sitting back. They must experience everything with both hands. In the beginning they've got to taste everything, and toward the end they've got to see everything you're talking about. They're always underfoot or thirty seconds ahead of you in the parking lot. It makes for an exhausting day.

War Wounds

Toddlers fall down a lot. They fall down everywhere. They trip over anything in their path, and if the path is clear, they'll trip over themselves within minutes. Consequently, they get the ugliest gashes and bruises on their heads, knees, and hands. People who've never had a toddler in the house may gasp and suspect child abuse, but a quick conference with said toddler's mother will confirm: "He's a boy. He's a two-and-a-half-year-old. And today he's a saber-toothed tiger." Nothing but business as usual here.

High Drama

The best actors surely must have memories of toddlerhood, when emotions run high, not to mention everything in between. Toddlerhood is fraught with drama of the most Victorian sort. At its apex, the most random things will set your toddler off. My daughter once had a complete Force Three meltdown because I put her Clifford the Dog book in the backseat with her instead of the front seat with me. Toddlers swing from the darkest pits of despair over spilled apple juice and then soar to giddy heights because Daddy comes home, all in the space of ten minutes. When shrinks invented bipolar disorders, they had toddlers in mind. The only time toddlers are blasé about anything is when they're ignoring you.

Leadership Qualities

Most toddlers are like cruise directors in training. They won't hesitate to tell you how to behave, that you should stop singing along with them, that you will not laugh when they speak, and that you are to serve them a second helping of strawberries. Now. This tendency toward bossiness increases as their vocabulary grows. One of my daughter's stock phrases is, "Watch me and do what I do." This is cute—until it's not, if you know what I mean.

Imagination Overload

Suddenly there are monsters in your toddler's sock drawer where there were none just yesterday. Your shoe has become a cash register, and an invisible dog is the reason your child always spills the milk at the breakfast table. Jackie's daughter recently crawled into the living room with a white towel over herself. Then she lay there for several minutes before her mom asked, "So what are you supposed to be? A ghost?"

"No," her three-year-old said. "I'm a diaper wipe."

Obsession

Autism—or toddlerhood? That's the question so many parents have when their twenty-month-old sons start reciting the names of every car Chevy makes or when their two-year-old daughters start hoarding pebbles. Toddlers do tend to obsess about strange things, and it's not for you to wonder why. Just try to indulge them if you want to fend off a tantrum.

Sometimes you can't even try. Once a toddler takes a notion to mind, there's no getting around it. Physical laws be damned.

My neighbor Emily was over once when her two-and-a-half-year-old daughter Magda saw a yellow gourd. "Orange!" she shouted. "I want an orange!" We tried to tell her that this wasn't an orange, but she wasn't buying it. Tragically, we didn't have any actual oranges, but that didn't deter her from insisting on one. Her cries for an orange worked into a frenzy, so we gave her the gourd, thinking she'd see that in fact it was not an orange. But the fact that she couldn't actually eat the gourd drove her even further into a tantrum. Finally, her mother wrestled her into her arms to take her back home, where she could try to switch the gourd with some real oranges. Who knew if this ruse would work? But it was our only option.

If toddlers are obsessive, they're also extremely literal-minded. If you mutter that it's going to rain cats and dogs this weekend, they won't budge from the windowsill until they see some. If you say you're so hungry you could eat a horse, they'll tell you they don't like horses—they want pasta instead.

Toddler Summit Tip

Think your toddler is strange? The odds are good that he's no stranger than any other normal, red-blooded toddler. A quick survey of toddlers in our courtyard revealed that all of them were obsessed with at least one activity that flummoxed their parents. Lydia moves furniture day in and day out. Yusef looks at books so long that his father has resorted to buying fancy toddler bikes and balls just to lure him outside. Chandler used to put every doll at her day care to bed at naptime, making sure each one had a mat and a blanket as well as a good-night kiss. Amir is obsessed with tools. Annie collected pebbles by the bucketful and kept them in little cups along her windowsill.

As the parents of this lot, we agree: don't wonder, just go with it.

The Difference Between Babies and Toddlers

Now that you've got a toddler in the house, there will be many days when you look back on the first year of parenting and wonder what your problem was. The biggest problem, of course, was your own gross ineptitude and inexperience, but lo, you did in fact come out the other side. Now you look back on all those anguished phone calls to the pediatric hotline or to your mother about how many teeth a four-month-old baby is supposed to have and chuckle. These days, parenting is a much more physical chore. And there's a lot more yelling involved. Let's look at some of the obvious differences between parenting a toddler and parenting a baby, shall we?

Babies Can Be Contained

You can swaddle a baby, or put a baby in a rocker, or put him safely in his crib. Even if he's in the midst of a heartrending cry-fest, he can't lock himself in the bathroom while he's having it. Toddlers, especially the older versions, have mastered not only their bodies, but also their environment, in alarming ways. They can unlatch the baby-proof cabinet locks and program the VCR. What makes you think they'll stay in their cribs?

Babies Can't Run Away from You

Not only can't you contain a toddler, a toddler's every impulse is to run like hell once she's escaped. This is another heart-stopping toddler trait that makes you yearn for the good old days when you could place baby on a baby blanket in the corner and expect to find her there when you next look at her in thirty seconds. Even if you had one of those babies who learned how to walk at nine months, they're pretty unsteady on their feet, making them very easy to catch. But a two-year-old will run from you the moment you let go of her hand—and in the worst, most hair-raising places: parking lots, the roofs of tall buildings, the zoo.

Babies Will Generally Eat What You Give Them

I sit and watch my friend Julia's one-year-old daughter Lulu eat, and I sigh and remember the days when my three-year-old ate the same way: with gusto. Lulu wants to eat and is genuinely happy to put *anything*, edible or not, into her waiting mouth. She screams with delight as she pulps bread. She gobbles down jar upon jar of fruit and vegetables. She actually seems to relish tofu bits. I once saw her snatch a whole grape out of her mother's hand and then wrestle her for it. She almost won, too, but her mom resorted to brute strength. Most toddlers won't eat a grape unless it's already a favored food and is the right color, of flawless make, and isn't touching any other food.

Babies Don't Talk Back

Need I say more?

Babies Don't Ask Why

Why? Because they don't have the vocabulary yet, most likely.

Why? Because their brains aren't as developed as toddlers' brains are.

Why? Because they're younger than toddlers, and they're not as smart.

Why? Because they're not as irritating as toddlers are with their incessant questioning.

Why? What are you? Some kind of existentialist?

Why? Because I said so, that's why.

Why? No idea. Go ask your father.

Babies Have No Fashion Sense

Babies will wear what you put them in. They have no say in the matter, and they leave it up to you to select the proper attire for the day. Toddlers, on the other hand, have a very highly developed sense of fashion. They will let you know, in no uncertain terms, what constitutes acceptable fashion fare, and what does not. This is cute some of the time, like on the weekends or in fair weather, when it really doesn't matter. But there will be many mornings when this tendency is tedious. Carrying your toddler out of the house clad only in her nightgown and the purple Barney boots she slept in is cute the first time. By the end of the week, though, your day-care provider may need to have a talk with you. But it will do no good. You'll quickly learn that if you try to influence what your toddler wants to wear, you'll only make the situation worse. Of course, your toddler also reserves the right to change his or her mind completely just as you've strapped him or her into the car seat for the morning, and you'll be forced to go back into the house for a complete outfit change. Remember, toddlers can accurately be compared to little rock divas.

Picking Your Battles

I don't know why the parenting books don't mention this. Maybe they do, but they don't ram it home. All toddler books should open with a two-page spread that says PICK YOUR BATTLES in thirty-point boldface type, and go from there. It is the prime objective of parenting toddlers.

Part of why toddlers are so, well, explosive, is because they don't know what they want. Or if they do know what they want, they can't procure it for themselves. A toddler's imagination is boundless and his socialization slim. From a toddler's perspective, there is much more being withheld from him than is being offered by this irritating, big parent person. They can't get to the steak knives. They can't reach the airplane up there in the sky. They can't drive your car. Imagine having your creativity constantly thwarted. A wall is big and white, thinks a toddler; why the hell can't I draw on it?

Alas, from your perspective, you need to somehow teach your tot right from wrong and keep him alive in the process. And so you spend your days fighting your toddler's inappropriate whims and desires. No, you can't have chocolate syrup to drink for dinner. No, you may not go to Grandma's wearing only your boots. No, you may not gift wrap the goldfish.

It's bound to wear you down. That's why parents of toddlers learn the most important lesson of all very quickly into the game: PICK YOUR BATTLES.

"Fine. Have ice cubes for lunch. But don't come to me when you're starving this afternoon."

By wisely picking your battles, it is possible to carve out a small bit of downtime for yourself. While your two-year-old is off playing with your cell phone, you can read the headlines, for example.

You also won't yell as much. As my friend Mimi has said about raising her toddler, "It seems all I do anymore is threaten and yell. My throat is always sore." Since a toddler's job is to vex you, you can spend most of every day telling them "no" to this and "get away" from that. If you try to fight them on everything, you'll age ten years in the space of two. You no doubt are already looking alarmingly older, and you're not interested in looking like Grandma before at least your fiftieth birthday.

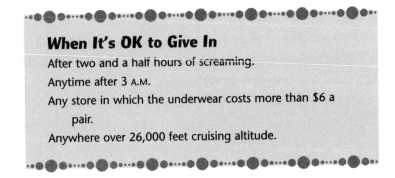

When It's OK to Give In

After two and a half hours of screaming.

Anytime after 3 A.M.

Any store in which the underwear costs more than $6 a
    pair.

Anywhere over 26,000 feet cruising altitude.

So how to preserve your peace of mind in the face of toddlerhood? Pick your battles.

In the world of toddler battles, there is wheat and there is chaff. You simply have to decide for yourself, based on your toddler's personality and your tolerance for artwork on the TV screen, how much you can take in a twenty-four-hour period. But how do you know which battles are worth battling? You'd be surprised how few actually are. Most of the biggies involve matters of personal safety and basic home-life routines you must insist upon in order to keep your sanity. Check the following Battle-O-Meter for a quick primer on what's worth battling versus what's not.

Battle-O-Meter

You're the mommy/daddy. You're bigger. You win these battles:

No running into the street or parking lots.
No playing around the swimming pool without an adult there to watch.
No touching the stove/heater/gas pipes.
No talking to/going anywhere with strangers.
No not sitting in the car seat.
No playing with the knife set.

Not life-or-death battles, but life will be better if you win most of these:

Clothing should at least be season-appropriate.
No ice cream for dinner (ditto breakfast and lunch).

Don't leave the table while eating.
Brush teeth before going to bed.
Bedtime at a regular time every night.
Three books *max*!
Only one drink of water per bedtime.

Fuggedaboudit! You can lose these:

Go ahead and play with my wallet.
Fine, go to preschool in your pajamas.
Yes, you can watch the *Rainbow Brite* video for the fourth
time this afternoon.
Yes, you can sleep in the closet tonight if you really must.
Sure, just bring along the umbrella.
If you can catch the dog, then you may dress the dog.

The Four-Way Path

Picking your battles wisely does not mean that you'll get
through the toddler attack without battles. By picking your
battles, you've only cut down the number of potential battles
by about 50 percent. What are you going to do about the
other half?

There are many other ways of handling your little explosive device, the four best of which I have helpfully culled for
you here. The first rule of thumb is this: when in doubt,
appear to give in to the toddler's demands. You don't really
give in to his every whim, of course, but you learn how to
exploit his weakness, optimize your superior IQ, and, as is
frequently necessary, utilize your superior brawn.

Take the time to learn some of these basics, and do it now. Since toddlers tend to get worse before they get better, it's best to master these tactics while your tot is still in the pupa stage—sometime soon after he's started walking and saying "no!" for example. Don't wait until you have a completely rigid two-and-a-half-year-old before you start implementing some of these tried-and-true methods of toddler management: diversion, negotiation, bribery, and brute force.

Oh, stop grimacing. These are toddlers we're talking about here!

The simple fact of life, and I believe I'm backed up on this by moms and dads with years of experience, is that you can't be progressive with a toddler. You can try, but asking a two-year-old boy to please not hit the cat in a gentle and patient voice is not going to get you anywhere. "I know you're feeling frustrated, Tyler, but you really shouldn't bite Daddy's leg like that," will not reap you the kind of results you want. Try these instead.

Diversion
A beautiful character trait of babies and very young toddlers is that they're eminently distractible. Sure, they want to draw on the wall and begin working themselves into a Force Three tantrum when you won't let them . . . but a quick cookie offering, an impromptu rendition of "Itsy Bitsy Spider," or the lure of another toy pulled from the pile on the floor makes them forget all about the wall.

This only works until they're two and a half, however. After that, toddlers become single-minded about things, and nothing you do can distract them from getting what they want. Here, by way of example, is a typical early-evening conversation with an almost three-year-old girl.

She: Mommy, I want a fruit bar.

Me: Sweetie, you just had a fruit bar. You can have another after dinner.

She: I want a fruit bar.

Me: Honey, wait until after dinner.

She: I want a fruit bar.

Me: What did I just say?

She: I want a fruit bar.

Me: No.

She: I want a fruit bar.

Me: No!

She: I want a fruit bar.

Me: No!

She: I want a fruit bar.

Me: I SAID NO FRUIT BAR!!!

She: Please?

Me: (feeling guilty) No, darling.

She: (a pause, then she releases the big guns) Why?

Me: Because I said so.

She: Why?

And so on.

You can see, then, that a hallmark of the older toddler is single-minded obsessiveness that is applied to everything equally, from books they want you to read to the food they want to eat. Why do you think the Teletubbies are such a hit with the toddler set? Because they understand this age group's love of the word "Again!"

Negotiation

When diversion ceases to work, it's smart to try negotiation. Negotiating with a toddler is dicey—it almost never works unless you're willing to accept a 60/40 agreement (60 percent on their side, I mean). But it can diffuse a tense situation because it makes the toddler feel like he's won the battle. Here's how it works:

> *Him:* Mommy, I want three candies.
>
> *You:* Nice try, pal. Finish your dinner.
>
> *Him:* I want three candies!
>
> *You:* No. No candy until you finish your dinner.
>
> *Him:* But I want candy! (the whining starts to pitch upward, and you hear a tantrum coming on)
>
> *You:* Tell you what. You have two more bites of your potato, and I'll give you one candy.
>
> *Him:* I want two candies!
>
> *You:* You'll have to eat all your potato for two candies.
>
> *Him:* OK!

At this point you might actually want to get the candy out and finger it in front of him so he has something tangible to work toward.

Bribery

When negotiations break down, it's a very quick slide into the depths of immorality, by which I mean bald-faced bribery.

Bribery, like wages, works wonders on all but the most principled sorts, which is to say that it works on virtually all toddlers. Parents should not hesitate to use it whenever necessary. All the books say that it will lead you down the slippery slope to a very unpleasant child who won't do anything unless something's in it for him. Maybe. But how is that different from the way most things work here in America?

Rightly or wrongly, I say you shouldn't worry about this one, because, and let me reiterate this one more time: bribery always works.

Now, bribery should never be the first line of defense. Let me be clear about that. First, you should simply ask your toddler to do whatever it is you need him to do. "Jason, let's go to the car now." Or, "Cindy, it's time to get ready for bed." You never know when your toddler is feeling charitable (or pretending he's a voice-activated slave robot) and is inclined to do as you ask on the first request. It's one of the rarest, most precious moments of childhood when your two-year-old actually puts her hand in yours and walks quietly down the street with you. It's just so unlikely it hardly bears mentioning.

Bribery works best when the problem at hand is getting your toddler from point A to point B. Working on the "carrot-before-the-donkey" model, a well-placed bribe can get a toddler into the car seat faster than you can say "Teletubbies." It will also get them to day care, home from day care, out of the candy aisle, upstairs for dinner, and into the bathtub. Of course, there are different kinds of bribes. There are really obvious, bad-mommy bribes, like the ones offered while trying to potty train ("This candy bar is yours to eat for dinner if you put your pee-pee into the potty!") to the more all-purpose, time-tested versions ("If you're good, Santa Claus will bring you a lot of presents this year.")

It's a bit harder to utilize the powers of bribery when negotiating a toy dispute. When Bobby and Suzy both want to ride the same tricycle, offering Suzy a juice box will only set Bobby off on a Force Two tantrum because he'll certainly want a juice box, too. Bobby may then try to push Suzy off

Parenting a Toddler (Schools of Thought)

I Understand You—Lots of modern parents try to deal with their toddler as a peer. This never works, because toddlers aren't peers. They're not even fully human yet. And face it, you really don't understand why a missing button should cause such screaming, do you?

Time-Out—On the assumption that giving a child a time-out when he misbehaves will keep him under control, parents spend most of the day and a large part of the night giving their toddlers time-outs. Works with varying degrees of success until about two and a half, at which point your whole day is one big time-out.

Let the Day-Care Person Deal with It—A professional's got more experience with this than you, right? It's out of sight, out of mind on the discipline question.

Because I'm the Mommy—Not very progressive, but it ultimately works. Why? Because you're bigger, mostly.

the trike, at which point Suzy will also start to scream, and then you have the dreaded toddler lock, and somebody will have to physically remove one of the offending parties or turn the hose on them.

Brute Force
Brute force. Dig it.

Necessary Stuff (Early Toddlerhood)

Good Wooden Blocks—A hundred different toys in one. A classic that your toddler will spend hours with, providing you with hours of rest.

Toy Kitchen—You can buy these used from families who've aged out of the attack or purchase them reasonably from any toy store. Since toddlers will occupy themselves with these for days on end, they're well worth whatever investment you make in them. Don't bother buying the plastic food they try to sell you with the kitchen—any normal toddler will create his own out of blocks, beads, dirt, rocks, or whatever else he can find in his room.

Decent Videos—I know, you promised yourself you wouldn't resort to this crutch, but trust me. There will be a night when you are ready to let your tot watch "Blue's Clues" five times in a row so you can make dinner.

Band-Aids—Very soon your little walker will begin to run, and then climb, and then dance, and twirl, and fall. A lot. Before the toddler years are behind you, you'll

Yep. When diversion, bribery, and negotiation fail, and you really have to get your toddler to do your bidding, brute force is your only remaining option, short of admitting defeat and walking away. By brute force I certainly don't mean beating the child to a pulp, although sometimes, God knows, the notion makes for pleasant fantasy. I mean taking advantage of your superior size to dominate an otherwise indomitable

have done your part to keep several large makers of bandages in business. Naturally, you'll have to buy them with Disney or Sesame Street characters on them. To a toddler's mind, there's nothing your kiss and an Elmo Band-Aid can't cure.

Cheerios—Small, crunchy, and familiar, there aren't many toddlers who won't eat these. Lots less sugar than, say, Cap'n Crunch Crunchberries.

Toy Stroller—Boy or girl, every single toddler gets off on pushing one of these little doll strollers. Considering how many hours of peace you'll get out of it, it makes sense to plunk down the $10 or so to buy one. But beware! Toddlers will attack each other to win possession of this coveted item.

Stools—You'll probably be sorry, but toddlers love footstools, which help give them a sense of the can-do. Unfortunately, this applies not only to washing their own hands but for getting the lollipops down off the high shelf as well.

situation. Every parent of a toddler knows what it's like to forcibly strap a screaming two-year-old into his car seat or drag an eighteen-monther away from the sandbox. Despite how it looks, these parents have simply had their hand forced by the toddler.

When a toddler is overtired, overstimulated, or underfed, she's likely to get so wound up that the only possible solution is to physically remove her from the situation. This is relatively easy to do at first, but less so later on, when your toddler is bigger and has a more violent temper. The hardest time you'll have with brute force is when your toddler has gone totally limp and you have to drag her out of the park under the scornful eyes of those parents who don't have toddlers yet.

If you're aghast at any of these techniques, clearly you're one of these parents. Stay tuned.

Translation Nation

One of the hallmarks of toddlerhood is a growing proclivity toward using speech to get what is wanted. Between one year and fifteen months, your baby starts replacing his points and grunts with a word or two. You'll be thrilled of course, because all parents count their children's growing vocabulary so they can proudly report it to the parenting posse back at the park. What constitutes an actual word is open to wide interpretation in the beginning. What sounds to you like "*Bonjour, Maman*" sounds more like "Buh-buh-buh muh-

muh-muh" to everyone else. Ironically, the more your child speaks, the less she is understood by others.

I chalk this up to context. A toddler very quickly goes from the realm of simple sentences like "big ball!" to providing you complicated instructions for what to do with said ball. Here's where you start to run into problems. Because a toddler always comes up with ways to utilize this ball, none of which have ever occurred to you. Not only do you have to decipher his imprecise language, you must also figure out what "ball," "computer," and "doggy" have to do with each other.

Ironically, after they've allegedly mastered basic speech, a lot of toddlers return to the world of grunts and points. Many add simple screaming to the patois as well as diverse dirty looks and snarls. Toddlers are masters at body language. Any one of them could put the famous mime Marcel Marceau to shame without breaking a sweat.

Consider this classic: she knows it's time for bedtime. You know it's time for bedtime. But like every night at your house, it's now the showdown at OK Corral. Your toddler stands in the hallway in her diaper, one arm akimbo, sucking insouciantly on a sippy cup while staring at you.

"It's time for bed."

No answer. Just that steely stare.

"Did you hear me?"

No answer. Suck. Suck.

You try your most commanding, adult voice. "I mean it, now. Come on! Let's go!"

Your toddler turns her back on you.

Suck.

When you make a move toward her, she'll break and run, screaming with either anger or delight, you can no longer tell which, until you catch her and forcibly put her nightclothes on. You might make the mistake of trying to be nice and giving her a choice between her Thomas the Tank Engine shirt or her "Blue's Clues" shirt, but you'll only get a grunt in response.

"Ungh-ungh."

Is that a "Choo! Choo!" like Thomas or a "Woo! Woo!" like Blue? You'll have to decide. Experienced parents know that either way you'll decide wrong and ignite a tantrum. The only good news here is that it's likely to be the last tantrum for the night.

I'll give toddlers credit for imagination—they are just learning the language, after all. But it doesn't make it any easier when they say one thing and mean the opposite. Toddlers strapped into car seats will demand to be "Let in!" when they mean let out, and they'll insist on a hard-boiled egg when what they really want is one scrambled. This naturally prompts many a tantrum after you've spent twenty-five minutes boiling an egg they have no intention of eating.

It also makes for a lot of surreal conversations. Annie recently asked me if she could go play on the chimney, to which I replied, "What chimney?" I wasn't about to let her play on a chimney, but first I wanted to know whose chimney she was talking about, since nobody in my apartment complex has a chimney. She kept insisting, growing more and more irritated, and acting like I was daft for not letting her go and do such a simple thing. We gawked at each other for some time until I realized she wanted to go out and play on the *balcony*. There's a two-and-a-half-year-old Egyptian boy in our courtyard who lectures his mother at length in a language nobody understands. "What's he saying?" I ask her, thinking it's Arabic. "I don't know," she says. "It's certainly not Arabic." I know another toddler who confuses the words *antelope*, *buffalo*, and *cantaloupe*, and uses them interchangeably. You can imagine the interesting breakfast conversation fodder this makes.

In late toddlerhood, you've got the added complication of imagination overload. Most three-year-olds don't live on this earth; they live in a fantasyland of their own design. If you don't take it upon yourself to learn the particulars of this fantasyland, you'll never be able to translate most of what your child is trying to tell you. It's up to you to know which imaginary friend your child is communing with this week, as well as the name of every doll, car, and rock he's found on the playground lately. He'll be talking about characters in the many nonparentally sanctioned videos he's been watching at day care, too, so don't be alarmed when he starts acting out skits between cartoon characters you've never heard of. "Mommy, you be Grog the Avenger and I'll be the Pink Power Ranger, OK?"

The older they get, the more attitude they cop at not being understood, so from a tantrum avoidance standpoint, it really is in your best interest to know your child's every nuance or get really good at faking it. You're always encouraging them to speak, right? You're always telling them to "Use your words" instead of the old tried-and-true whine or mini-tantrum. So from a toddler's point of view, as long as they're using words to communicate, you damn well better understand what they're telling you.

Trouble is, it's hard to decipher messages from a fantasy world you're not invited to. You never know who or what's inhabiting your toddler's body at any given moment, and you're risking a grave tantrum if you guess wrong. My neighbor Misti tells me her son Amir changes form several times nightly.

"Amir, please take this to the bathroom," she tells him.

Amir won't move. "Mamma, I'm an elephant."

"OK. Elephant, please take this into the bathroom."

"But Mamma, I'm a baby elephant."

"OK, little baby elephant, please take this into the bathroom."

"You have to put that on my back. I don't have hands." (Yes, this little boy is extremely loquacious.)

After his mother has somehow fastened the object in question onto his back, he'll happily lumber off into the bathroom. Fifteen minutes later when she calls for the elephant again, he won't answer, because now he's a puppy.

Care also must be taken to watch your own language use when the little ones are about the house. Toddlers are notorious mimickers. They parrot everything you say, and they're *always* listening, even when you're sure they're not. They're listening as you drive home from the doctor's office, muttering to yourself about what an %%$*& he can be sometimes. They hear you badmouth the %$ yuppie in the $##**! SUV who just cut you off. They listen to you and Daddy berate the !!@*@! at work and their %*?% ideas. It's funny, then, how surprised you'll be when you hear such salty language coming forth from their little lips and wonder indignantly where they were exposed to such filth. From you, baby. From you.

There are several methods you can try in the hopes of increasing the percentage of utterances you ultimately understand. All of them are flawed, but as with most things toddler, you have to make do with what you have.

- **Force them to speak more clearly.** If you're a masochist and love continual household drama, then this is the route for you. Of course, your toddler will do everything in his considerable power to thwart you in this effort, probably to the point of not talking in coherent sentences at all. Ask yourself if you really need to do this to yourself.

Four Toddler Phrases That Will Shake Your World

1. **No.** Comes early, often before the first birthday. Never a good sign, because it means that baby is developing a mind of his own.
2. **Mine!** This includes his toys, his food, and most of your possessions. Don't bother trying to argue.
3. **Why?** Expect this to be the question of your every waking hour from ages two and a half through three. Why? Go ask your mother.
4. **I hate you.** OK, not just one word, but three doozies that indicate your child is moving out of the toddler years and into the much more manipulative preschooler set.

- **Guess.** This one is hard to pull off without setting off a huge tantrum because, in general, you have only three chances to guess what they're trying to say before you disgust them entirely. This option is too much like a multiple-choice exam for my taste. "The goldfish is (a) real, (b) red, or (c) dead." Good luck.

- **Pretend to understand them.** Using a variety of generic, noncommittal responses like "Wow, honey. That's great!" Or, "Ha-ha-ha! You're so clever!" usually fools a toddler for a while. But by the third year, every toddler knows when he's not being listened to, and that's when they start breaking the crockery to get your attention.

- **Just say no.** Usually your safest bet.

Now that you know what you're up against, you need to be aware that you're also going to have to seriously up the parenting ante to survive. Unfortunately, your life as a parent takes on ever more rigid parameters as you take your child through the toddler years. In a sense, it makes you a slave to the particular character traits of this stage. You don't want a public tantrum, do you? Then you'll take certain precautions. You want her to eat something, so you agree to buy the only food she seems to be interested in—string cheese. Don't chafe; it's a temporary condition you're taking on as you quietly mold her more into your own image. Are you ready? Take a deep breath. Make another pot of coffee. Here we go.

2

SLAVE PARENTS FROM BEYOND INFINITY

*"My kids would never eat anything
unless they saw it dancing on TV first."*
—Erma Bombeck

Toddlers, like babies, come in all different flavors and personalities. If yours was a mellow baby, then you'll probably get a reasonable toddler (although nothing is ever guaranteed when it comes to toddlers). God forbid you had a more feisty infant. Colicky, highly strung babies tend to mutate into the kind of toddler you need a stun gun to control. But even with a mellow toddler, you'll have to suffer through your fair share of tantrums, public scenes, and circular arguments you can't win. No parent ever makes it through the Attack of the Toddlers unscathed. It's just a matter of degree.

As a parent, you're forced to mutate yourself merely to adapt. This is necessary for survival, and, not unlike the tactics employed by the denizens of a deserted island on a certain hit TV show, most of them aren't very pretty. None of these necessary changes have anything to do with what the books say about handling your toddler. Indeed, trying to raise a toddler "by the book" means you'll just be that much more guilt-ridden as you're forced to scream and yell in order to cope with your rampaging toddler. You can "discuss the issues" with a toddler until you're blue in the face. I can guarantee you the toddler won't be listening.

Those of us who've lived through the Attack of the Toddlers know this to be true. You'll have to learn a whole new skill set to survive these next few years. These are tried-and-true tactics that everyone who's ever been in your sneakers has employed, to mostly satisfactory results.

Grinding Routine

One of the first lessons you have to learn when dealing with toddlers is that routine is next to godliness. Toddlers are creatures of habit. They want to wear the same shoes, carry the same toy horse, eat the same breakfast, lunch, and dinner every single day, and be read exactly three books before bed and then get their kiss, without fail. This applies even though they tell you very earnestly that they don't like the routine. They don't want to go to play group this morning! They don't want to have a nap! They don't want a bath and they don't want you to read them a story. You need to learn early on that they're only fighting you on principle, and that if you actually listen to them and pass on one of these events, you'll suffer for it greatly.

A standard toddler tantrum:

Tot: I don't want macaroni and cheese for dinner!
You: OK. What do you want?
Tot: I want rice!
You: So be it. (you dish out a bowl of rice, which you just happen to have on hand)
Tot: No!!! (throws himself to the ground)
You: What's wrong now?
Tot: It's not macaroni and cheese!

It's one thing to assert their independence, as long as their safe and well-known routine stays the same. Remember, every toddler reserves the right to change his mind.

Knowing that toddlers live by routine, it's possible to train them into a routine that works around your schedule. By twenty months, a young toddler is starting to get anal about what he wants out of his day. He wants his morning schedule the same every day, so get him used to getting up at 7:30, having a few minutes of snuggletime, then his diaper changed, then his bowl of Kix and cup of juice, then his clothes put on, and then out to the car to drive to day care. Don't vary this routine, and he'll come to rely on it so much he'll hardly fight you. Best of all, he'll think it's his routine when it's really yours.

It works with food, too. Get them used to certain kinds of food in the months when they're still eating widely and you'll be grateful down the road when their diet suddenly takes a turn to the anorexic. I didn't introduce Annie to peanut butter and jelly sandwiches early enough, and by the time she was two, she refused to eat sandwiches of any kind. This causes a problem at day care (although my day care provider is willing to sub her sandwich with eggs and apple slices) and anywhere else where one relies on mobile, neatish foodstuffs.

A toddler's daily routine often takes on the ridiculous attention to detail that calls to mind Dustin Hoffman's character in *Rain Man*. Not only are there just certain foods they'll eat in the morning, there is certain cutlery to use, certain bowls, and particular cups. You'll have to get the same kind of milk or your toddler will rebel and refuse to drink anything at all. It doesn't matter that they can't read yet—they know what the carton looks like. They want to watch the same TV shows in the morning. (Once kiddie channels realized this, they saved millions in new programming costs.) They want to go to the same park and go down the slide three times and swing on the swing for ten minutes before moving to the climbing fort. It's chicken noodle soup or nothing at lunch. They'll fuss before naptime, but you both know it's expected. The rest of the day progresses in the same measured fashion. Day-care providers have recognized the importance of keeping to a routine, and if they successfully use it to corral four or five toddlers at once, then you know it will work for you.

Spelling Skills

Toddlers have keen ears. They are always listening, particularly when they are in the next room or pretending to be otherwise engaged in play. Since there are all sorts of incendiary topics that must be avoided if you want to avert tantrums or constant pestering, you must learn to spell.

Everyone with toddlers knows that if you even so much as pass a M-c-D-o-n-a-l-d-s your tot will insist on a H-a-p-p-y M-e-a-l every fifteen seconds until you relent. You know that all she's going to eat are her f-r-i-e-s and her C-o-k-e, and that she already has five of those B-e-a-n-i-e B-a-b-y octopi cluttering up her room. So you try to bribe her into eating the fish sticks you have at home by promising her ice cream, which you just bought today at the store. She'll vehemently oppose this idea, but by now you're almost home, so you force the issue. She starts to have a tantrum because she wants a Happy Meal, with the same dinosaur hand puppet that Jason has. Sorry, you tell her, no Happy Meal tonight, and you curse Jason's mom under your breath for being such a profligate yuppie and buying her spoiled brat son anything his little heart desires. You endure her despairing cries until you get home, at which point she refuses to get out of the car. As you stand there debating whether to leave her there or forcibly carry her to the house, your neighbor comes by and you explain to him that clearly your little D-A-R-L-I-N-G didn't have her N-A-P today and that B-E-D-T-I-M-E will come early tonight.

Objects of Compulsion

To live with a toddler is to live with a small obsessive-compulsive.

New Knowledge

Remember when you didn't know what a binky was? Or a bouncy seat? Or syrup of ipecac? Just as you learned a whole new vocabulary when your first baby was born, you must now tap into whole new areas of knowledge, much of them very specialized, all of it heretofore unknown to you. But don't worry. Your toddler will teach you.

This is terribly unpolitically correct to admit, but a lot of toddler interests divide along gender lines. This isn't always the case, of course, but it is often the case. I didn't do it, Nature did, so blame her when your son decides he will only play with trucks from the time he's two onward. Boys tend to go more for the categorization than girls. They're the ones who will throw a tantrum if you call a Jeep an SUV. The difference matters to them. This is the sort of compulsion that leads men to

Toddlers obsess. When they discover something new, they must examine that something from all angles and carry that something around for a week and collect every subcategory of that something. It can be endearing to see how fervently they throw themselves into new knowledge. It can also be tedious. Even hellish.

A friend with a four-year-old tells me that last year her son was obsessed with *The Grinch Who Stole Christmas.* "He's never even seen the video, but apparently he's seen the commercials for the movie. Now he grills me about the Grinch all

alphabetize their music collections in their twenties. Girls, on the other hand, seem to want to collect things. Rocks, for example. Or green-colored things. Or crayons. What does this say about women? I'm not even going to go there. . . .

Here are some standard objects of toddler obsession:

Trucks—You'll have to learn the difference between an eighteen-wheeler and a semi.

Tools—Any two-year-old can tell you there's a difference between a Philips and a flathead screwdriver.

Dinosaurs—This is what boys used to memorize ad nauseum before Pokémon came around.

Horses—Don't complain when your toddler starts to collect horses. Just pray she stays at this level and doesn't start asking for a real pony.

night long. 'Now, why did the Grinch steal Christmas, Mommy?' Well, because he had a stone heart. 'Why did his heart turn into a stone?' And so on. I'm going to rent him the video, but I was hoping to make it past Thanksgiving first."

Last year he watched the *Barney Christmas Special* four times a night, every night of the week, for months, she tells me. One night her husband could take it no longer. He threw the *Barney Christmas Special* outside in the trash can. That lasted about thirty minutes, she tells me, until he was compelled to go back outside and root around for it to restore peace and harmony to the household.

I'd take the Grinch any day.

Slave Parent Powers

Got toddler? Then you've got these new magical powers, too!

The Kiss of Life—Your kiss can now heal all ouchies, from the most invisible scratch to some pretty serious hurts. Even if you have to take your child to the doctor, God forbid, this kiss of yours will help calm him or her down.

Monster Master—You alone have power to seek out and destroy all monsters in your toddler's room each night. Wield this power benevolently, and you and your child will sleep more soundly.

Sock Smoother—Somebody has to smooth the bumps out of socks and tights, right?

Toddler Support Group

You remember how important your new parent friends were? They were the ones who arrived on Planet Parenthood at roughly the same time you did. They wanted to hear all about your new baby's strange rash, and they were always up for comparing stroller brands. In the scary, early days of new parenthood, you clung to each other like life rafts in a deep new sea.

But as you grew more confident as a parent, you might have drifted away from them. Some of them you lost once the terror of being a new parent wore off and you realized the only thing you had in common was a delivery date. Others left town in search of affordable housing, better jobs, or superior school districts.

Hopefully, you kept some around, however. It's important to keep in touch with your parent friends, because if ever in your life you needed empathetic people around you, it's now.

Parents of toddlers don't judge you when your twenty-monther throws herself to the floor of the restaurant because she didn't want sauce on her spaghetti. They know how to handle bites, pushes, and toddler locks when two or more toddlers want the same toy. They understand why juice boxes, alphabet cookies, and goldfish crackers in plastic baggies are commodity items. They're an invaluable source of new techniques for getting toddlers into the bath, into bed, or out the door in the morning, and they're always ready to shower your toddler with the kind of compliments he really wants to hear.

"Say, partner, those are *some* cowboy boots! You look like the roughest, toughest cowpoke this side of the Rockies!"

Allying yourself with other parents of toddlers is one of the best ways to make it through the Attack years mostly intact. It's always easier to get through your day when you have somebody to compare notes with. While there's still a certain amount of comparative parenting in the toddler years, by and large it's become more a matter of bonding together for safety. Toddlers all do the same general things—tantrum throwing, picky eating, boot wearing, grime collecting. But the details are usually variations on the theme. One toddler likes to draw happy faces on compact discs; another prefers to torment the family pets. With a group of other toddler parents, you can feel secure in knowing that no matter what your tot did last night, it was probably perfectly normal. It's always reassuring when somebody else can top your story, too.

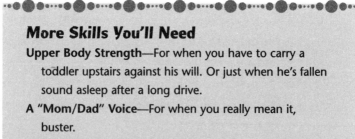

More Skills You'll Need

Upper Body Strength—For when you have to carry a toddler upstairs against his will. Or just when he's fallen sound asleep after a long drive.

A "Mom/Dad" Voice—For when you really mean it, buster.

Patience—For when they're not interested in getting dressed this morning.

Imagination—For when you need to talk to the invisible goat or kill the sharks in the carpet.

Ideally, you want some toddler parent friends in close proximity, because then you will be able to share resources, both emotional and household.

Say one morning you wake to find that you're out of Cheerios, which is your toddler's traditional morning cuisine. You'd meant to run out the night before to procure some more, but in after-dinner and the bath/bedtime follies, neither of you could muster the energy needed to drive to the store. So you forgot about it, and now your toddler is about to pad into the kitchen and find her morning routine savagely altered.

On your own, I'd say you're in for a bad morning. But if you have a toddler parent friend in the vicinity, you can make a quick call, and chances are, they have an extra bowl of Cheerios they can bring by. You'll owe them big if they do, of course. But then you'll think nothing of slipping them your new *Toy Story II* tape when the day comes that their copy breaks.

Toddler parent friends also make excellent resources of new information. Pick any toddler problem—tantrums, refusing to wear clothes, refusing to eat anything but ice, and more than likely, one of your friends will have a suggestion you haven't heard of yet.

Last summer I was telling a group of my neighbors that getting my daughter to take a bath was akin to strapping her onto the conveyer belt at the sawmill. Everybody nodded, empathizing. A few hours later, one dad knocked on my door. He had with him a little bottle of tablets that turned bathwater different colors. "This," he told me, "will get Annie into the bathtub. Guaranteed." It worked miracles on his kids, he said.

Sure enough, that night, as Annie geared up for her evening scream-fest, I nonchalantly opened the bottle and tossed a few tabs into the bath in her full view. "What was that?" she said, actually venturing into the bathroom. "What are you doing?" I told her I was turning the water purple. Did she want to get into a purple bath? The little tablets fizzed alluringly at the bottom of the tub.

She couldn't get her clothes off fast enough. I told my neighbor my entire Disney video collection was at his disposal.

Clearly, these people are of great value to you in your new circumstances as the parents of a toddler. But where do you find them? By the time babies turn into toddlers, their parents have split neatly into two camps—those who are back at work full time (hence, their tots are being dealt with by professionals) and those brave enough to go it alone at home (hence, they're running their toddlers at the park).

Back when your child was a baby, meeting new moms was mostly an exercise in finding other women home with a small baby who were both available for coffee and dressed as badly as you were. Now that your toddler is more, ah, personable, it's gotten more complicated. Not only do you want to like the parents, you need your kids to like each other.

That's relatively easy if your kids all attend the same preschool or day care. The kids already have their pecking order and run in a pack. And the parents don't have to hang around with each other any longer than the few hours the occasional birthday party or holiday gathering requires.

If you're at home, however, or live in a community with lots of toddlers around, it gets more complicated. Toddlers must be parented in the most aggressive sense of the word. Every parent has a different way of parenting, just as every toddler has a different way of thwarting that parenting. The trick is to find parents whose parenting methods you can stand who also have toddlers your toddler gets along with. Get what I'm saying?

An example: Say you have neighbors whose little girl is about the same age as your little boy. But their little girl is a biter and a screamer, while your son is the sort who's destined for an M.F.A. in poetry one day. To make things worse, her parents subscribe to the "I Understand You" mode of parenting—that is, they never yell, they never physically remove, they empathize. This empathy has turned your little boy into a human chewbone whenever your neighbor's daughter comes over for a play date. If you agreed with her parents' parenting methods, you might all be able to get along. But since you don't, you spend the afternoon fighting your urge to drop-kick this kid when she starts in with the chompers. It won't be long before you'll be making elaborate excuses why you can't have them over to your house anymore. You don't like the girl, and you don't like the parents, because their kid hurts your kid and they won't do anything about it.

Best to find another toddler who matches your own in manner and outlook and pair them up. Two biters will scare each other into an understanding. Two book lovers will sit quietly together for hours. Two chasers will happily go at it with each other long enough for you and her mommy to share a nice cup of coffee and a Danish. It hardly matters if you two adults get along. Your collective relief will be enough to bond you.

Play Date Etiquette

Once upon a time, people grew up, married their high school sweethearts, bought a little house in the old neighborhood, and raised their kids. The women all stayed home and knew each other, and on summer days the streets were filled with screaming, happy neighborhood kids running amok.

These days most of us have to make do with the play date.

For those of you lucky enough to not know what a play date is, it's just what it sounds like. You make an appointment with another mom or group of moms (sometimes even dads) to get your kids together to play. It's a sad by-product of this age in which small children not even out of diapers have busy social calendars. Between Kindergym and music classes and swimming lessons and mom's group, who has time for play anymore? Especially if you don't know any of the neighbors, assuming the neighbors even have children.

But play dates can be good things. If you can find a group of moms you can tolerate and a well-matched group of tots, the community can grow and thrive and benefit everyone. Plus you'll have something to do on rainy days.

First, you'll have to find a group of moms to join. It's often not too hard. Hanging out at the local park will often get you an invite to join a play group already in progress. Once you've been invited, take pains to make a good first impression. Bring along something very tasty to eat, or buy the coffee (the way to most moms' hearts is through their stomachs). Try to have your toddler rested, fed, and in whatever state he's least likely to bite anyone.

Now that you're in an established play group, here are some more general rules of thumb:

• **Pack it in, pack it back with you.** In other words, clean up after your toddler and try to leave the house as you found it. Go ahead and put the dishes into the dishwasher to help out the host. Don't forget your sippy cup or your baggie full of apple slices. If your toddler hid his cookies under the couch, clean them up before you leave. Pat down your toddler to see if there are anybody else's toys on his person.

• **Volunteer early and often.** A good group will self-destruct if everyone doesn't pull her weight. Volunteer to arrange the snacks for a month, or arrange the birthday celebration that month. Rotate the host-home and include your own. If it's too small to handle everyone, get everyone to the park instead when it's your turn to host.

• **Keep it real.** Remember, you're the alleged adults now, so when one kid is acting out, don't gang up on the kid or his mom; discuss what you can do as a group. Keep it mature, now. No *Lord of the Flies* situations, please.

• **Attendance is next to godliness.** If you don't go, the toddlers don't bond, and the other moms won't cotton to you, either. You'll get the reputation of a flake, and you'll have wasted everybody's time. Your toddler will whine more, too.

Tapping Your Inner Toddler

Life with a toddler isn't a life built on reason. You soon learn that toddlers have a belief system unique in the world and that your pedestrian adult values have almost no place in it. To get through to him means, most of the time, tapping deep into your inner toddler.

What does this mean, you ask? It means exactly what it sounds like: stomp your feet, pout, hold your breath, whine, cry, and refuse to budge when told to.

"I'm not moving this car until you get into your car seat."

"I can't hear you until you ask nicely."

"You'd better be nicer to me if you want any more juice."

Getting on a toddler's level is not something sanctioned by most of the books, and yet it is usually remarkably effective. Toddlers universally recognize the physical factors that keep you in authority—you're bigger, stronger, and faster—and as such, they pay you grudging respect. It stuns them into submission when you start acting like them, too.

Phrases Slave Parents Love
Wash 'n' wear
Velcro
Two-for-one Cheerios
Child menu/family-style restaurant
Priced to own

Rachel and her friend Chloe were playing in Chloe's mom's living room. Being the two-year-olds they were, they both wanted to play with the doll crib, and soon there was a bad case of toddler-lock, replete with screaming and tears.

"You two need to take turns playing with the crib," tried Rachel's mom, Linda.

"Rachel will put her dolly in first, then Chloe can put her dolly in," said Chloe's mom, Kate.

Neither Chloe nor Rachel let go of the crib.

Since toy battles had been going on from the moment the play date started, neither mom was up to any more attempts at responsible parenting. So Chloe's mom grabbed the crib.

"That's my crib," she said. The girls stopped screaming and stared at her, too surprised to speak.

"No . . ." started Chloe.

"It's MY CRIB," said Kate. "And I'm taking it into MY bedroom so NOBODY can play with it." She removed the coveted crib from the room. Naturally, the girls began to whine, but their hearts weren't in it, and they soon lost interest and turned their attentions elsewhere.

It works, I tell you. And in addition to working much of the time, it makes you feel good by giving you an outlet for mini-tantrums of your own.

One dad I know actually threw his screaming two-and-a-half-year-old into the tub fully clothed (gently—don't worry) after she'd changed her mind about taking a bath one too many times. "I'd just had it with her attitude," he told me. "So I decided to get on her level."

Did it feel good? It sure did, he reports. "She was a pleasant person the rest of the night, and I was a happy daddy."

Of course, tapping into your inner toddler isn't your first option, either. I've discovered that a parent has to venture deep into the toddler years before they figure out that it's a viable option. When your child is just entering the Attack mode, say at around eighteen to twenty months, he or she is really too young to understand that by stamping your feet you're not acting as you normally would. Instead of wasting a perfectly therapeutic tantrum, count to ten instead and continue on with more adult methods. By two and a half, however, your toddler is more evolved, and as such, much more aware of the alarming nature of your actions.

One week when my then almost three-year-old daughter was sick, I let all of my normal household rules lapse in an effort to make her feel better. I let her watch videos during the day. I let her eat Cheerios in the living room. I bought her several Happy Meals. I let her sleep with us. By the middle of the week, she was physically all better, but mentally she had turned into a surly tyrant. I let her stay home Thursday for good measure, and she continued to milk me for all I was worth—cookies, Happy Meals, endless video viewing, and no bedtime enforcement. By Friday morning I'd had quite enough. I announced that she was well enough to return to day care and asked her what she wanted for breakfast, Cheerios or Kix? She announced that she wanted a Happy Meal and she would not be getting dressed, nor would she be going to Sandra's, her day care lady. I asked her again to please get up, pick out some clothes, and come out and eat her breakfast. She told me to shut up and get out of her room.

Now, I work from home. My assignments were piling up and no money was coming in, and darn it, I needed the girl to get back to her friends and her routine at day care so I could get back into my routine. She had other plans, apparently. I could see this was going to take drastic measures.

"I'm going to ask you one more time," I growled. "Cheerios or Kix?"

She stared me in the eye. No answer.

So I had a tantrum.

"FINE!" I yelled. "YOU DON'T GET ANY BREAKFAST AT ALL!!!"

Yes, it was quite a scene. I threw stuffed animals around the room. I forcibly got her out of her nightgown and changed her diaper, which I then threw into the hallway. I pulled clothes out of the dresser and put them on her. All the while I yelled about how I was the MOMMY, damnit, and I took care of her while she was sick and I deserve to be RESPECTED and HOW DARE she treat me like this. "Now COME ON RIGHT NOW—WE'RE GOING TO SANDRA'S—or do I have TO CARRY YOU TO THE CAR, TOO?"

It was clear I meant it. I was speaking the toddler language of absolutes.

"Mommy," she squeaked. "May I please have some Cheerios first, please?"

"Yes, you may," I said, panting. She ate her cereal without spilling a drop. She announced politely that she was done, and thank you, and that she was ready to go to Sandra's. We walked hand in hand to the car, and I only had to ask her once to get into her car seat.

Did I squelch her joie de vivre? Of course not. By that evening she was feeling safe and secure, back into her routine, and was easily able to talk me out of washing her hair during her bath.

It's a Toddler Thing

One of your most important jobs as the parent of a toddler is to guard that toddler's special sleep toy. Most kids by this age have become attached to some object they habitually

To Bite or Not to Bite?

Got a biter? We've been there. Unfortunately, the Toddler Summit can't come to any concrete conclusions about how to tame them. Some parents say it's best to tap deep into your inner toddler and give your incorrigible biter a modified chomp right back. That way you show him in a manner he understands that biting hurts. Others disagree, and warn that biting a biter back will only scare him or drive him into an uncontrollable rage. And you don't want to handle *that* without special gloves. Take your toddler's personality into consideration before deciding what to do. Be careful!

comfort themselves with. This can be a doll, a stuffed animal, an old blanket, even one of your old T-shirts. Dr. T. Berry Brazelton calls it a child's "lovey." I'll call it their "thing."

Your toddler will drag this thing all over with him. It will become very worn and very dirty. Even if you're not inclined to let a little dirt bother you, eventually this thing will get so grimy you'll be compelled to launder it. Your toddler won't be pleased. First, it will be out of his hands for the period of about one hour. Second, when you return it to him, it will no longer smell as it did, and a major tantrum will ensue.

Many parents make arrangements to buy a shadow thing, a thing identical to the thing their toddler sleeps with, so that they can alternate this thing with the other thing when that thing needs washing. An alternative thing can come in especially handy should you lose the original thing outside. Are you following me? In this age of mass production, you'll probably be able to buy an identical object for your toddler and have it on hand for just such emergencies. For this reason, it's never wise to let your toddler get too attached to a unique, one-of-a-kind thing.

At some point your toddler, who is very attached to this thing, will want to take it outside with him. He'll beg. He'll cajole. Finally, he'll insist. Be swayed at your peril. Understandably you'll probably cave in once the screaming starts, but try to dissuade him, using any means possible. Remember that if you step outside with this thing, it's in your best interest to guard it like it was the Hope Diamond.

Why? I'll tell you why. For something that's so integral to your toddler's well-being, he's surprisingly sanguine about it. He'll leave it in the park, at the store, at day care, and in the car. If you're traveling, your toddler will leave it on the bus. He'll leave it on the train in a foreign country where you don't even speak the language. Notice that sinking feeling as the train's pulling away? That's your stomach.

Yep. Even though your toddler doesn't seem to pay a lot of attention to this object, it is in fact very important to him. It's his security object, and it represents a little slice of home and comfort to him. When he goes to hug it and finds it no longer there, he goes all a-twitter and doesn't know what to do. And we all know what toddlers do when flummoxed, don't we? They start to scream.

You won't get an ounce of rest until you've found the thing.

Moms and dads of toddlers around the world have tales to tell of hunting for their child's thing in the dark backyard with a flashlight in the dead of winter, of calling the airport and hoping the cleaning crew turned in a soiled, peach-colored dinosaur to lost and found. My father-in-law once drove across London in the rain because my daughter left her dolly at her great-grandma's house.

Luckily, many, many people in public positions have had to deal with toddlers, and so are aware of the consequences of tossing away any lost items that might possibly have belonged to a young child. Most airlines will collect all manner of stuffed animals and ratty blankets out of airplanes and hold them, anticipating your anxious midnight call. Taxis will, too. Restaurants, libraries, even other parents in the park will recognize the object left behind as a thing of great import to a little child, and will either hold it for you or place it safely on a bench for you to reclaim when you return. Because as everyone who's ever had a toddler knows, you will return.

In the House of the Rising Tot

We've talked about what toddlers do to your head; now let's talk about what they do to your home.

When your child turns into a toddler, your home life once again mutates into something that would have given you second doubts way back when you were trying to conceive. It's true you've already baby-proofed the place and removed all fragile objets d'art or other tasteful remnants of adult life that your baby might have harmed himself with. But as baby gets older, his ability to get to these items, as well as his creative scheming in doing so, grow as well. Therefore, you have to remove just about everything you ever liked from your living room or risk losing it to your toddler's curious (and slippery) hands.

At about two years old, toddlers learn about stacking, for example, and about the properties of leverage. This means they can do lots of cute things like make a block tower. But it also means they can make a tower out of your CDs, or your books, or cups and plates with things still on them. They'll empty out the salt and pepper shakers to see if salt and pepper stack. Then they'll figure out that they can "stack" themselves on chairs or stools and get to almost anything you don't want them to. The day you walk into the kitchen and see your two-and-a-half-year-old standing on a kitchen stool with her hands on the cookie jar, it's time to upgrade your baby-proofing scheme to toddler-proof, at which time you can just kiss household order and tidiness good-bye and embrace the coming chaos for the next couple of years.

Your kitchen ain't the same, either. You've got two sets of dishes—yours and your toddler's. Your food pantry starts to look like a 7-Eleven store—filled with processed food, gallons of milk, and goldfish crackers by the bucket—because these are things toddlers consider comfort food and you consider acceptable baksheesh. Sometimes, the only way to get your three-year-old out the door in the morning is to hand him a baggie-full of goldfish crackers as a bribe. Moreover, no toddler will ever have what you're having for dinner, so slowly your grocery list begins to mutate to include the kinds of food you haven't tasted since you were a child. Fish sticks. Peanut butter. Popsicles. Microwavable chicken patties shaped like ducks. Sure, sometimes you can keep your toddler ignorant of these kinds of foodstuffs, but only as long as you keep him or her away from other toddlers. Once they go to day care, it's only a matter of time before they experience their first Pop Tart or their first Happy Meal, and then it's all over for you and your attempts at keeping them organic. They won't look at another Tofu Pup until they're in college.

The backyard, if you're lucky enough to have one, is also a shadow of its former self, what with all the garishly colored plastic swing sets and climbing structures strewn around. The plants are all dead, the flowers all plucked, and the sand from the sandbox has killed most of your grass. The lawn furniture you got for your wedding is just too heavy and sharp-edged to be safe around impulsive toddlers, so you packed it away in the garage. The pets long ago took up residence under the house, and for all you know they've been dead for months. At least that cuts down on the amount of dog or cat poop your tot might otherwise be inclined to hide in his overall pockets.

Maybe you thought you'd get your house back again once your baby grew out of the oral stage. I'm sorry, but didn't I mention that once you have children in the house, it becomes their domain until they run away or leave for college? Tragically, it's true. And once again, there's nothing you can do about it. So just put away the Pottery Barn catalog for now, because that leather couch you're pining for just ain't in your near future.

Becoming the Parent
You Never Wanted to Be

Real parenting starts in the toddler years. Hopefully, by this juncture you've realized that the idealistic, progressive parent who doesn't believe in spanking or yelling is going to get eaten alive by any toddler worthy of his peer group. Or maybe you haven't. It doesn't matter. Your hand will be forced no matter what school of parenting you subscribe to. No matter how patient you are, no matter where you got that child psychology degree, no matter how much you think you know how to handle this age group, you'll lose. You'll turn into a yelling, finger-wagging, head-shaking, 100 percent exasperated parent by the end of the Attack or wake up child-free and realize it was all a horrible dream.

Toddlers do this to you. They simply find your level of irritation and up the ante until you crack. They find all your buttons, and then they push them. It's not their fault really, it's just their way of making sure everyone understands that they're not babies anymore. They need to find out just how far you can be pushed so they can grab that much more independence for themselves and then toe the line menacingly while keeping you engaged.

Five Kinds of Toddler Parents

The Screamers—Parenting by vocal cord. Like ugly Americans in a foreign country, these parents have decided that the reason their two-year-old is ignoring them is because they must not be able to hear them. The louder they scream, the more deaf their tots become.

The Slaves—When their tots bark, they jump. Their policy of no yelling, no spanking, no anything that might squelch the free spirit of their precious little toddlers has resulted in their indentured servitude. Slave parents are often seen at the twenty-four-hour supermarket buying Popsicles at 6 A.M.

The Drones—In war, the term for this is *shell shock*. Nothing the toddler does gets a rise out of these

Of course, they'll never admit this. And because they're so good at pushing your limits, you're apt to start seeing it as some vast, right-wing conspiracy to drive you insane. But that's just toddlers doing their job. Naturally, you're forced to become the kind of parent you never wanted to be. What else can you do?

When I say that all parents of toddlers turn into the kind of parents they never wanted to be, you know what kind of parent I'm talking about. The woman dragging her limp two-and-a-half-year-old through the parking lot. The man trying to coax his twenty-monther out of the toy store. And then there's that poor woman in the grocery store. Remember her?

---

parents. They've been pushed too far, and now they've snapped. Will they ever come back? Good question.

The Clowns—Will dance for their dinner—their toddler's dinner, that is. Exhausting to watch, these parents keep their tot amused through a never-ending series of physical pratfalls. Straws up their noses, handstands, bleating like sheep, anything to keep their toddlers from starting to scream. Easy to spot, since the transition back to the adult world is difficult.

The Defeated—The toddler won. You'll recognize these parents by their haggard appearance and their resignation to spend all afternoon with their two-year-olds making Play-Doh cakes while listening to Raffi.

The one with three kids in the basket? One's broken a bottle of apple juice on the floor and wants to play with the glass. Another is ripping open every box of food in the cart, grazing as she goes. The third has probably pooped his pants and is crying for attention. The woman looks like a homicidal psychopath and is screaming at her brood. Everyone in the store who has not yet experienced unique psychosis that comes with toddlerhood regards her in horror.

A friend recently sent me this joke via E-mail: A lady is in the grocery store pushing her toddler in the cart. The toddler is screaming and crying. The lady is muttering, "Stay calm, Rachel. Don't cry, Rachel. It's OK, Rachel." Another woman passes by and remarks, "My, somebody is very patient with Rachel."

The mom glowers at her. "What are you talking about?" she says. "I'm Rachel!"

The only way you'll avoid becoming this woman is if you have the sense never to take three children under five grocery shopping without adult backup.

By the time your child is almost four, your parenting style will have dramatically changed and will bear no resemblance to what you thought it would be. You're just not able to listen to your toddler's every imaginative yarn, no matter how clever. You can't stay calm when he decides that no food is perfect enough to put in his mouth. You will end up throwing away just a fraction of that artwork she brings home every day, if only to free up some wall space in the kitchen. These and many other scenarios are what make the difference between a parent who doesn't have a toddler and a parent who has a four-year-old. This isn't anything to be ashamed of. It happens to most everyone. Just accept your fate and join the crowd.

Morsel du Jour

Nobody knows why. Nobody knows exactly when. The only thing parents who've survived the toddler years know is that at some point between fifteen months and three years, all kids abruptly stop eating.

This is typically cause for great concern among parents, most of whom remember the turmoil over introducing their young to solid foods in the first place. Babies who ate broccoli and strained prunes with gusto just a few weeks ago suddenly and inexplicably decide that these and most other items are now off the menu forever.

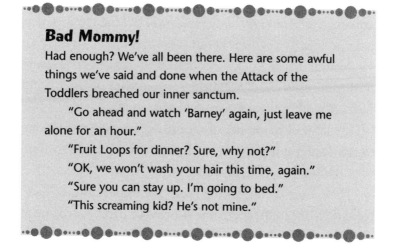

Bad Mommy!

Had enough? We've all been there. Here are some awful things we've said and done when the Attack of the Toddlers breached our inner sanctum.

"Go ahead and watch 'Barney' again, just leave me alone for an hour."

"Fruit Loops for dinner? Sure, why not?"

"OK, we won't wash your hair this time, again."

"Sure you can stay up. I'm going to bed."

"This screaming kid? He's not mine."

Two things happen. At about one year of age, most babies suddenly lose interest in eating so they can concentrate on more pressing matters, such as walking. This freaked you out, because you were used to shoveling food into your little bird's mouth as fast as you could spoon it out of the jar. But then, in the next few months, as your baby became more and more sure on his feet and started yelling "no!" at every opportunity, something else happened. Your baby mutated into a toddler, and before you know it, he's objecting to food because it's the wrong color. Or because it's touching other food on his plate. Or because he no longer approves of the texture.

This extreme punctiliousness about food is so textbook toddler it's become a cliché. Nevertheless, it's guaranteed to manifest itself before the toddler years are out, so you'd better get used to the idea. Any day now you'll serve your toddler a dinner that was perfectly acceptable yesterday and the day before, only to have him push it away in disgust. What happened? The experts wring their hands and prattle about growing autonomy and independence, but the truth is, they have no idea what this is about.

No number of books or seminars you attend on "How to feed your picky child" will help you feed your picky child. In the end, you're on your own. And as is usually the case, you'll begin to devise a number of sneaky ways to get your toddler to eat—every one of them an affront to the rational method of parenting you were planning on.

Here, once again, let me recap the importance of good feeding habits to the mental well-being of parents. It's one of those universal, primal things: when your kid eats well, you feel good. In terms of button-busting pride, watching your toddler snarf down a whole bologna-and-cheese sandwich and a giant glass of milk ranks right up there with winning the Nobel Peace Prize.

But at some point you would swear on a stack of Bibles that all your two-year-old has eaten in the last week is dry toast, and you start to wonder how he'll react to the IV drip the doctors at the hospital will start him on once you bring him in.

Strangely enough, this rarely happens. The experts swear up and down that this loss of appetite is natural. And indeed, I happen to have living proof that such habits do not hurt the toddler. My own little brother was a pudgy baby and a voracious eater until he hit three. Then, according to my mom, he abruptly stopped eating and became rake-thin. To this day he remains tall and thin, but then he also surfs daily and has something like 1 percent body fat.

The kind of food a toddler in full-on food rebellion deigns to eat is always a surprise. My friend Thea coined the slogan, "If it's white, it's all right," meaning that her daughter Natalie would eat only white, highly processed foods like Wonder Bread, instant mashed potatoes, and white rice.

Fortunately, most toddlers have one thing they'll eat that almost constitutes good nutrition. My daughter will fall apart if I put even butter on her pasta, but she'll eat a whole raw carrot at the grocery store. Lulu will eat anything with ketchup on it. Alex and Lisee's son Alec ate peanut butter and jelly sandwiches. It was PB&Js for breakfast, lunch, dinner, and all in-between-meals snacks. Lisee tried to sneak other nutrients in there. She tried slipping various flat vegetables. She tried hiding melted cheese under the peanut butter. Nothing worked. In the end, she had to content herself with switching the fruit variety of her jelly and remind herself that peanut butter, after all, does contain protein.

Here are some common household foodstuffs that are highly suspect in your toddler's eyes.

Sauces—Too strange and lumpy for most toddlers, although sometimes ketchup is acceptable.

Herbs—A total toddler turnoff. In a toddler's eyes, all seasonings are dirt and therefore not edible. This is strange, because up until recently, a lot of young toddlers were very much into actual dirt from the backyard.

Butter—Usually OK for bread and pasta, but still unacceptable for some diehards (like my kid).

Spices—Usually too much like dirt to interest a child. Besides, it introduces too much flavor into a dish, which is also a bad thing.

Sandwiches—These are usually OK, as long as they are scrupulously prepared (crusts removed and the rest cut into triangles).

Vegetables—Never an acceptable food option.

Scared yet? Don't give up hope. There are several methods for trying to deal with this strange, toddler phenomenon, none of which will ultimately work. But you're free to try. Write me if you have any success.

Creative Cooking

Find the three foods your toddler will eat and rotate them creatively. If junior will only look at cheese, toast, and grapes, well, then consider yourself lucky. You can make several creative meal options out of those three items. Whole segments of the publishing industry are known to live on the cheese and grape platters they find at book parties and gallery openings, and if they can thrive, so can your toddler.

Try a Happy Meal

Look, I hate to even suggest this, and I swear to you I am not in the pocket of the McDonald's Corporation, but it does seem to be onto something here. There isn't a toddler I've come across who won't eat Chicken McNuggets or a bag of fries. Especially when they come with a Power Ranger or the dinosaur toy every one of the neighbor kids has. Of course, if you go this option, you have to significantly downsize your definition of nutrition. But if your toddler seems to eat nothing but ice anyway, this can be an attractive alternative.

There are several other downsides, though. Once your child has tasted the dark fruits of the Happy Meal, you will never again be able to drive past a Micky D's without your toddler screaming for you to stop the car and having an ugly meltdown when you don't. One mom I know actually tells her toddler that McDonald's is closed for much of the week, and she often takes an alternative driving route just to avoid having to explain why there are people inside the restaurant. I almost hate to tell her that her ruse won't work very much longer. No three-year-old will fall for that kind of thing, and she'll have to come up with ever more elaborate lies—like telling her daughter that the elves who make Happy Meals went on strike. Or something.

Try Bribery

Another painful option, but one that not surprisingly begins to work after around the third birthday. Eat ten more black beans and one more bite of your tortilla, we tell Annie, and then we'll give you some more Coke in your cup. She counts them, naturally, and will have nothing more to do with her taco until we give up some of that Coke, but she at least has that much more nutrition in her belly, right?

Consult Outside Sources

If your toddler eats nothing but bread at your house, make sure you ask his friends' parents what, if anything, he'll eat at theirs. Ask your day-care provider as well, since most times peer pressure does funny things to a picky eater. Seated at a small table with their friends, they'll eat things they'd never eat at home. You can also gain valuable insights into what your kid likes that you might never have offered. I recently found out that Annie loves hard-boiled eggs. "She'll eat two at a time," her day-care provider tells me. Well, who knew?

She stopped eating scrambled eggs a long time ago, so I stopped making eggs for her at all. This new revelation was very useful, since now I had a guaranteed source of protein in my arsenal of acceptable Annie foodstuffs. I learned she loves cucumbers from our neighbors, a Chinese couple who eat them sliced on hot summer days. Seems Annie can't get enough of them when she's over playing with their son Daniel. She refuses to eat the steamed carrots she all but lived on a few months ago, but she'll eat most of one large sliced cucumber. Go figure.

Keep Trying

I haven't experienced this for myself yet, but people tell me that eventually most older toddlers begin to segue out of this picky eating stage and back into the realm of the noshing. The trick is to continue making a variety of foods available to them. So they loved carrots until they hit two years old, then they refused to allow them on the same table with their cup of ice, and then finally, they deign to make another nibble and find them acceptable. By some accounts, however, you have to offer them this unacceptable fodder something like forty times before you can expect them to try it. The lesson here? Shop economically.

Since you'll have to deal with this phenomenon for three or more years, chances are you'll be forced to adapt your own meals to more closely resemble what your toddler's having. This often means more simple fare—pasta has saved the lives of millions of toddler families—along with the kinds of food you haven't had since you were a kid: fish sticks, peanut butter and jelly sandwiches, Pop Tarts.

There's good news, however. Nutritionists have assured me that, all evidence to the contrary, most toddlers do in fact get the nutrition they need to sustain their level of growth and energy. The trick is to look at what they consume over a week instead of a day. And toddler portions are really very small. If you can get your tot to eat a bowl of grapes while he's watching his *Thomas the Tank Engine and Friends* video, he's had his fruit for the week. Ultimately, toddlers have their own best interest in mind. They'll let you know when they're really hungry. And when they're really that hungry, they'll broaden their tastes just enough to include what you're having.

Eating Out with Your Toddler

The toddler years are all about looking back on your first year of parenthood and remarking on how simple it all seems in retrospect. Remember how you could take your baby to a restaurant and she'd fall asleep next to you in the car seat? Remember being able to set her down and return to find her in the same place after ten minutes? Of course, all that went the way of the dodo once she started walking. And as things with your toddler got worse and worse—the spills, the tantrums, the refusing to eat anything with any color or nutritional value—you probably figured you could kiss your days of dining out good-bye.

You can dine out with a toddler. I've seen it done. I've done it myself. It just requires a few new twists on the theme. You have to patronize certain eating establishments that only just meet the legal definition of restaurant. You shouldn't expect to eat much yourself. Assume that several beverages will be spilled and dress accordingly. And it helps to go as a team, because four hands are better than two when it comes

How Do You Get a Picky Toddler to Eat?

"We have a rule in our house that you have to at least try it before you can say you don't like it," says my neighbor Linda, mom of a five-year-old and a three-year-old. It works, but the trick is, they started this rule early, so her kids accept it as the unquestioned norm.

Misti does it another way. Once upon a time when her son first started exhibiting picky eating tendencies, she would spend all evening cooking any morsel he requested just so that he would eat something. One evening, she recalls, she prepared six different meals. Amir turned his nose up at them all. "So I learned the hard way," she says. "And I backtracked fast." Now she makes whatever she's having and puts Amir's portion on the table. "He'll ignore it for a while," she says, "until he realizes that's all he's getting. Then he'll come and eat."

to mitigating the mess your toddler will leave in her wake. Eight hands are even better.

There is a Mexican restaurant in my neighborhood that is patronized by every family with small children for fifty square miles. It's a big, open place, with lots of booths and tables with places for car seats and high chairs. The food is good, and most every kid views rice and beans and tortillas as acceptably edible. It's also cheap enough that you can shrug off the $4 you spent on a plate of rice and beans your toddler has eaten one spoonful of. Because it's considered a family restaurant, people without kids recoil from the chaos and din of the place. Pizza places are also usually toddler-prone. Some diners are as well. Denny's, for example, is already loud and brightly colored, making it possible to camouflage your kids. Plus it has a nice kid's menu featuring things like hot dogs and grilled-cheese sandwiches.

Once you're at an eatery that won't throw you out for making a mess, proceed to eat. Younger toddlers are more dicey to deal with, because they're still interested in throwing food and letting cups of the non-sippy variety slip from their grasp. They're approximately three times as messy as older toddlers, who are generally better with the cutlery but just as apt to spill their drinks. You'll spend more time mitigating full-scale food fights with younger toddlers than with their older brethren, but you'll spend more time trying to get your older toddlers to concentrate on eating. Either way, it's a wash for you.

Prepare the scene. Attach the bib and hide the knives. Blow out any candles placed on the table for mood, since nobody here is relaxed, anyway. Make sure you have straws, and pour out half your toddler's beverage so he can sip from his straw without spilling most of said beverage into his lap. Remove all offending olives from the pizza. Make sure you offer her a slice that is free from burn marks or strange burned cheese growths on the crust.

Take a deep breath. Are you ready?

Eat. No, not you. You'll be too busy with damage control. Wait until your toddler is finished, then ask the waiter to put yours in a doggy bag so you can enjoy it in peace tonight after your toddler is asleep.

Depending on how hungry the toddler is, he may take as many as two bites on his own before trying to get out of the booth and under the table. Coerce him into staying with simple voice commands, resorting to diversionary tactics if necessary. You'll of course have remembered to bring a small toy. The finest family dining establishments have their own crayons and paper for just this purpose. Get him to take a few more bites. Save the threat about no dessert for last.

Make sure you have plenty of napkins ready for when your toddler spills his drink all over his pants. Note I said "when," not "if." Experienced parents bring not only a whole roll of paper towels with them to dine out, but several dry changes of clothes as well.

Remind them that if they want any ice cream, they must take another bite.

With older toddlers, you'll have to contend with whatever magical creature they are at the moment the food appears. For me, this involves telling my daughter that even though she's a tiger, she cannot put her plate on the floor and eat from it. And she's got to use utensils, too, unless it's a hand-eaten sort of food, like pizza.

With younger toddlers, it's not so much the imagination as the overall chaos. I recently watched my friends Julia and Javier do the dinner out thing with their young toddler, Lulu. It was an elaborate dance with Julia trying to keep Lulu from upending the bowl of soup while Javier wiped the soup puddle up around the bowl. Lulu would reach for her sippy cup, then get interested in a nearby butter knife, which her father would snatch out of her hand. As she'd start to yell, her mother would offer her another bite of soup, hoping she'd take it out of the spoon and not dip her hands into the bowl instead. Then Lulu would drop her cup on the floor, and as her mother dove to get it, she'd sink both hands in the soup bowl and squish the contents between her fingers. Her father would then try to clean her up just a little, bribing her with a piece of tortilla, which Lulu would suck on, then throw back at him. Then she'd tip the whole soup bowl over and lunge for more tortillas.

See why it's important to only go to places that are equipped to deal with situations like this?

No one would blame you for not going out at all until the child is four, either.

Toddlers: The Real Capitalist Tool

As you soon found out when you first had this baby thing of yours, there's nothing a marketer likes more than a new parent. Your name mysteriously found its way onto all manner of mailing lists and subscription cards, and suddenly you were finding cases of formula at your doorstep or diapers in your mailbox. The great marketing database in the sky compelled you to buy, and you did, willingly, for the benefit of your helpless new baby.

Now that you've got a toddler, your prowess as a shopper has tripled. Not only has your desire to make your progeny happy gone unstilted, but now your progeny can make specific requests. And he *will* make requests. And the older he gets, the more specific they'll become.

Toddlers are little sieves of culture. I read somewhere that an anthropologist can tell where a child's been raised by the age of three. By that time, all the cultural ticks and mores have been ingrained enough to make that toddler a good little Englishman, or Japanese, or American.

And so while an English toddler already enjoys tea and milk in the afternoon, your American toddler enjoys getting you to spend money on her. She's watching "Nick Jr." in the mornings, either at day care, or at home, because by this time you've caved and started turning on the TV so you can look at the newspaper and gulp your coffee in peace. She knows who Little Bear is, and Franklin, and Arthur. She loves Dipsy and La La, and she not only wants the dolls, but the sheets and the wall posters and the stickers and so on. She's already a good little American, digesting the media and consuming appropriately—with your help, naturally. Are you going to deny your son or daughter another educational *Sesame Street* video when you grew up on it? Of course you're not, and everyone knows it.

So you turn into the kind of consumer that brings a tear to a marketer's eye. You shop with abandon, especially when you can justify it *for the good of your child*. When Disney announces that *Pinocchio*, for example, will be available on store shelves for a *limited time only*, you jump. You race down to the video store and you buy that video, just to ensure that your child has a copy of it. Did you ever give a thought to Disney after your high school grad night party? I sure didn't. But now the company is very much part of my life. I was all set to boycott Disney because I didn't want to play any part of the marketing juggernaut it's become. But because I have a toddler, I'm their slave. We have a large video library of Disney classics and an equally large collection of the cheaper part II knockoffs. Disney also owns the *Winnie the Pooh* franchise (a fact that enrages my English husband, who made sure his daughter got a set of the original A. A. Milne Pooh books from his grandmother in London), so most of what she sleeps on, eats off of, and wears is a covert Disney endorsement. Even though she's preliterate, she can recognize the Disney trademark and logo on a billboard from a quarter-mile away (and she doesn't yell "Disney!" she yells "Winnie the Pooh!"). She's got her Lion King underwear and her Little Mermaid toothbrush. Every time she has spaghetti, we've got to reenact that silly *Lady and the Tramp* scene, both of us slurping on the same piece of noodle until we meet in the middle and kiss. Sigh.

To Buy Toys or Not to Buy Toys?

If you found it impossible to resist buying your baby every little bangle and book you came across, you'll find your VISA bill tripling with a toddler. Because they're so much more developed, they can enjoy so much more in the consumption of toys. Musical instruments, art supplies, tricycles. It's hard to go shopping at all without finding something you know your budding architect or Broadway star would love.

And yet I submit that, toddlers being the gelatinous balls of undiluted imagination that they are, you could stop buying them toys altogether, and they'd never notice. Nor would their development be impaired in any way. In fact, you'd probably improve it. I know several kindergarten teachers who have observed a decided lack of imagination on the part of five-year-olds who have grown too used to SuperNintendo games and other fare that blinks and flashes and otherwise does the playing for them. A toddler should be able to play for hours with one pack of crayons. Observe your own toddler, and tell me it's not so. Here are a few items you probably have lying around the house that will occupy any toddler for hours, if not days:

- **Boxes.** A good box is better than any toy in the known universe to a toddler. That's because it can become anything in the known universe, from a cave to a car to a table to serve tea on to a giant robot that conquers the world. Serves as a cozy bed, too.

- **Plastic measuring cups.** The best bath toy ever invented.

- **Rocks.** I don't know what they do with them, but toddlers collect them by the hundreds.

- **Kitchen tongs.** The possibilities are *endless*!

- **Laundry basket.** Empty or full, it doesn't matter. Your toddler will find something to do with it that doesn't involve washing or folding.

- **CDs.** They stack, and you can see your reflection in them, plus there's a neato little rainbow reflection. Need I say more?

- **The cat.** Why yes, those *are* dirty looks you've been noticing from your cat.

- **Your wallet.** And when you need your credit card to pay for a client dinner in a few weeks, just remember that the reason it's no longer in your wallet is because it's now under the hall rug.

- **Flashlight.** Hide the one you really use for emergencies unless you want your toddler to ruin that one, too.

Before you had a toddler, you might have wondered (but probably not) why Disney would pull certain videos off the market for a few years, while re-releasing others. The truth, as I see it? It's a twisted but brilliant scheme to let the next generation of toddlers come of whining age. My daughter saw *The Little Mermaid* at a friend's house once and begged for it so pathetically that one of us went soppy and bought it for her. Now she sings those sappy songs to herself day and night, and I find myself searching for bootleg copies of *Beauty and the Beast* on eBay because you can't buy it in stores.

Is there a trip to Disneyland in our near future? You betcha. We'll buy her mouse ears and a T-shirt and an Ariel the Mermaid doll. Not because we want to, you understand. I'd rather spend $500 on a trip to Hawaii. But because we're her parents, and we're balancing the desire to give her this cultural experience with keeping her from having a meltdown on the monorail.

You're headed for the bigger-ticket items soon as well, if you didn't already succumb last year. The toddler years are when you really start to see the sense in a minivan, or at least a station wagon, with lots of cargo space, built-in car seats, and one of those coffee cup holders in front. Your grocery bills are also a growing concern. You have one shopping list for yourselves, and an entirely separate one for your toddler, filled with the kinds of things only he'll eat. The next time somebody offers to add you on to their discount warehouse membership, you'll pay attention to the procedure. A zoo membership is handy to have for all those Sundays when you want to get the kid out of the house but don't know how far you'll get before meltdown. Washers and dryers. Fluffy pets. Swimming lessons. The list of things you blithely slap down your plastic for grows as your kid does.

Shopping No-No's

Your shopping habits are one of the first things to change when you've got a toddler in the house.

- Never take a toddler into a Toys "R" Us. Not if you ever want to see the light of day again.

- Avoid the candy section at all costs. If you have a legitimate need to buy candy (for Halloween, for example, or for your own personal stash), hire a babysitter, and hide the product well.

- Even if your toddler has never laid eyes on a TV, try to avoid the movie tie-in promos at the front of the store. She knows who Woody, Buzz, Barney, and Bart Simpson are, even if you think she doesn't.

- Feed your toddler before you go grocery shopping.

- Unless you want to eat every other meal at McDonald's, don't introduce your child to a Happy Meal, no matter how hungry or harried or tired you are.

- Never utter the words "happy" and "meal" in the same sentence, unless you're desperate enough to go to McDonald's.

- Never assume it's too early for Pokémon. Especially if there are older kids around.

- Never assume your toddler hasn't pocketed something. Shake her down before you leave unless you want to set off the shoplifting alarms.

Most parents I know would agree that parenting babies is a cakewalk compared to parenting toddlers. After reading this chapter and comparing it to your own experiences, I'm sure you now agree. But you might as well get used to it. There's a few more years of this stuff down the pike. You've still got lots of work to do in terms of civilizing and taming your little beast. Oh yeah, and did I mention the potty training? Stay tuned.

The Taming of the Beast

3

"We don't know what we want,
but we are ready to bite somebody to get it."
—Will Rogers

And lo! In the beginning, there was the baby. And all was good.

Then the baby learned how to walk and started learning how to talk and to point. And he began to show great emotion when spoken to or admonished thereof. And he began to desire, nay, demand, all manner of objects, both great and small, and would like unto a warrior gird his loins for battle when these objects he received not. And he would take neither food nor drink, nor would he slumber. And among the family elders there was great wailing and gnashing of teeth.

If it walks like a duck and quacks like a duck, then it's a duck, as the saying goes. But this isn't true of toddlers. They walk like people and they talk like people, but they're definitely not people. Not yet, anyway. Not by a long shot. And this is where you come in, Mom and Dad. Somebody has to take this walking contradiction, this tantrum-throwing, impulsive, irrational, self-obsessed being and turn it into a member of society who doesn't throw her Chicken McNuggets out the window of a moving car. We're talking civilization here, folks.

Normally, when we think of civilization, we think of what happened when hunter-gatherers settled down and started cultivating crops and domesticating dogs. But in the parenting sense, civilization means taking the steps to rein in the unchecked aggressions and inappropriate desires of your quasi-person, breaking him down and remolding him into a smaller version of yourself. This means potty training. It means teaching him the routines of the household, basic hygiene, family traditions. It's not an easy job, but somebody has to do it.

And you said you'd never turn into your parents.

Discipline and Consistency

But more to the point, what this job entails over the next two or so years can be summed up in two words: discipline and consistency. You need to be on much more than just a nodding acquaintance with these two words. To civilize a toddler, you must be deliciously intimate with these words. In short, you must tack them onto your refrigerator door and live them. Daily. If you don't, you risk creating a monster you'll have to live with for the rest of your life.

Believe it or not, your toddler wants to be tamed. He'll thank you. His future therapist will thank you, too.

Discipline didn't much come into the game back when you had a baby. There's no point in lecturing your three-month-old, since all he would hear was the same thing as that famous Gary Larson cartoon, "What Dogs Hear" ("Blah blah blah, Larissa. Blah blah! Mommy blah blah, Larissa.")

Comparatively speaking, the first year was a cakewalk compared to the second and third years. Disciplining the under-one-year set mostly meant admonishing your seventh-monther not to bite Mommy when nursing or asking the eleven-month-old to refrain from throwing food. Baby wasn't going to run into the street, because for the most part, baby was in your arms or locked safely in her stroller. Even when she first began walking, you kept on her tail religiously when outside.

Discipline starts to be important when a baby gets enough physical prowess to run away from you. This ability, combined with her shining new ego and ability to debate whether or not you're really serious when you say, "Stay on the curb," makes for a dangerous package. Should she listen? Or should she just run for it? Hopefully, you've managed to instill just a kernel of discipline in her emerging sense of self, enough for her to realize she'd better stay on the curb.

Hopefully, you've also learned how to read her face well enough to take the appropriate action when you see your orders are about to be ignored.

Some people dislike the word, not to mention the notion of, *discipline*. This is because they see it as some kind of cruel, soul-crushing damper on the natural exuberance of toddlers. But nobody's talking about locking your kid in the closet every time he pulls the cat's tail. I'm talking about the kind of basic adherence to rules that will keep your toddler from ending up in the middle of the street under an SUV.

He or she has to know when you're joking and when you're serious. He has to learn better than what his toddler impulses are telling him to do, and it's your job to help him. He has to understand that he never, ever goes into the street without holding an adult's hand. He has to learn about sharp knives, hot water, mean dogs, strangers, and the dangers of running with his shoes untied. It's this kind of training that helps ensure your toddler grows to adulthood, at which time he'll get to inflict such constraints on his own toddler.

Consistency is a little easier than discipline in most (but not all) cases. You might have gotten a little taste of consistency back in the first year. It came into play when baby started sleeping through the night finally, and the two of you began to wrap your lives around the idea that baby went down each night at 6 P.M. no matter what. No matter who invited you to dinner, no matter who was on the phone, when evening rolled around, it was bathtime, then bedtime, so that Mommy and Daddy could have some semblance of a life together. This was more for your sanity than your baby's. Now it's for both of you.

Consistency is a two-edged sword with toddlers. On the one hand, toddlers themselves are creatures of habit. They want to be fed the same foods at the same times in the same bowl as the night before. On the other hand, it seems to be written into toddler DNA to fight you tooth and nail on all matters that involve your attempts at consistency.

All toddlers develop a diabolical repertoire of stalling tactics and use every one—in rotation, so you don't catch on—before bedtime. They'll list six good reasons why they can't go to day care this morning, starting with "I don't want to" and ending with "But I wore those shorts yesterday, so I can't wear them today." You have to constantly remind yourself that even while they're trying to foil the daily routine, they'd really flip out if you let them.

Taking a mile when you're given an inch seems to be an important toddler coda. That's why you must stay the course no matter what. If you let them eat dinner in front of the TV just once, you'll never hear the end of it, and they'll know you're not really serious about eating at the table as a family. If you let them stay up past their bedtime every now and then, they'll know that bedtime isn't set in stone. Toddlers know there's the announced bedtime and the real bedtime—that nebulous hour between when you really start yelling and they actually pass out on their own.

But, of course, we can't be consistent all the time, unless we're really anal or married to U.S. Marine drill sergeants.

There can be exceptions with good reasons—we just have to make sure these reasons are clearly spelled out. For example, we don't watch TV during the day. That's the rule. It has to be dark before the idiot box ever goes on. The exception? When Annie is sick and stays home, then she can watch videos.

Consistency, while overall a settling thing, plays a strange role in your relationship to your toddler, because it applies to everything in life, not just household routines. For example, my neighbor Linda recently cut her long black hair into a sportif little pixie cut, which got rave reviews from everyone except her three-year-old boy, Mason, who acted like she'd abandoned him on the interstate and refused to look at her for days. You'd think it was his hair she'd lopped off so dramatically. But, of course, to his mind, it was his hair.

Toddlers are funny like that. As you'll quickly learn, there are a whole host of things you'd be safer off by not changing for two or three years. These include, but are not limited to,

- **Homes.** No moving during the toddler years, if you know what's good for you. Move when they're still an infant, or wait until they're four. Otherwise, you're in for it.

- **Furniture.** A toddler version of Hell: They go to day care or preschool like usual, and when they come back, *everything in the house looks different!*

- **Facial hair.** My friend Gene had long hair and a beard until his daughter was two and a half years old. When he decided to go square—actually, he says, he just got tired of all the hair in the shower—he cut it all off and presented his new clean-shaven self to his family. His wife loved it. His daughter ran screaming from the room and wouldn't let him near her for days.

- **Crockery.** If I can't find the "magic spoon," a regular spoon with rune-like marks on the handle, I might as well not even serve dinner to my daughter.

- **Pets.** God forbid little Snowball should die.

- **Another sibling.** Uh. This requires a whole section. Keep reading.

Obviously, you'll have to endure a certain percentage of tantrums based on things like changing seasons, visiting relatives, and new clothes, but that can't be helped. It's all part of life with toddlers.

In the meantime, you two have to calm down. You must start implementing the sort of household regimen your mother had back when you were a small child. Remember whining about how unfair it was to have to go to bed even though it was still light outside? Remember fighting baths? Remember being scrubbed for church on Sunday mornings? This was all part of the expected routine, and it didn't matter whether we liked it or not—that's the way it was. Toddlers need regular schedules. If their inner lives are in emotional turmoil and their bodies are suddenly able to do all sorts of scary new tricks, then at least they can feel safe in the routines of their home turf. It's your turn to be this kind of stalwart killjoy. You're the grownups now, even if you don't quite believe it.

Year of the Potty

If ever there was a reason for parents, potty training is it. Who else would ever take the time and energy it takes to convince a baby to put his bodily waste in the proper place? No one I know. Yet this embodies the spirit of parenthood, and we dutifully do what we must to nudge our progeny toward this most basic of civilized behavior. We do it with a smile on our faces, too (OK, maybe that's a grimace), as we look forward to the day when we can scratch the $20 jumbo diaper pack off our shopping list.

During your first year as a parent, potty training seems about as far off as the SAT exams. But like dentist appointments and work deadlines, the time to begin sneaks up on you and taps you on the shoulder to remind you that, hello, you're already running late. For a lot of parents, myself included, potty training seems like the first concrete test of our parenting skills, and so we spend a great deal of time avoiding the issue until it's all but upon us, and our toddlers are standing before us as we sit on the pot, asking, "Mommy, what are you doing?"

When to introduce your child to the concept of putting his bodily output into the officially sanctioned receptacle is a question the experts can't agree on. These days, most experts say a toddler is ready to start learning anytime between eighteen and thirty months, but this age range has been creeping upward for decades, and even now is in a constant state of flux. A 1935 publication by the U.S. Children's Bureau said that toilet training should "Always begin by the *third* month and be completed by the eighth month." It also instructed mothers on how to use a soap stick "as an aid in conditioning the rectum." In our mothers' day, the timing of potty training had significantly loosened up, so to speak. But most kids in the United States and Europe were still potty-trained by eighteen months. It was a scandalous reflection on your parenting skills if your child was still in diapers by age two.

But in 1962, Dr. T. Berry Brazelton published a study of 1,100 patients suggesting that later potty training, say, between the ages of two and three, led to fewer problems later in life. (No word on exactly what those problems were, however.) The age children potty-trained began to inch up. Today, it's not uncommon to find children two, three, and even four still running the streets in diapers. There's even a new size six diaper for kids who weigh over thirty-five pounds.

But this has gotten out of hand, critics say, and now there is a push toward earlier potty training once again. Brazelton got into a highly publicized snit with psychologist John Rosemond over when to potty train in the pages of the *New York Times*. Brazelton, who strongly advocates waiting until the child decides he's ready to potty-train, came under attack from Rosemond, who says it's a parent's job to train the child on the parent's schedule. With most families working full time and day-care centers refusing to take tots still in diapers, few parents have the luxury of waiting three or four years to get their progeny onto the potty. Parents teach their small children to drink from cups and use silverware, right? Better to step up to the plate and teach them this most basic of social skills. Rosemond also noted that Brazelton, who is a spokesman for Pampers, has lots of financial incentive to keep kids in diapers as long as possible. Brazelton pooh-poohed this idea, and said this kind of "tough love" approach to potty training ignores everything experts have learned over the years about children's motivation and self-esteem.

For his part, Rosemond developed a method of toilet training he called "Naked and $75," meaning that if you take a week off of work, stay home, and let your child run around naked, at the end of that week your child will be potty-trained. The $75 is what you'll spend cleaning your carpet.

The *New York Times* "toilet wars" were the buzz of parenting groups around the country. And with good reason. Potty training is one parenting duty that's easy to get obsessed with, many months after you've stopped being obsessed with every little milestone your baby reaches. The whole household starts to revolve around it, and for several months, it's all you think about.

Woe betide anyone who asks you how your child is doing while you're buried deep in these trenches. You'll launch into a detailed discussion of what your son must be thinking when he hides behind the living room chair to poop, or why your daughter doesn't seem to mind sodden diapers even though her friend can't bear them. You'll tell him excitedly about the big poo-poo in the potty just last night. You'll relate the cute terms your toddler uses to describe his poop and pee to you. He'll be forced to listen to you gush about how your daughter just learned to wipe herself, and all manner of private family details he doesn't want to know about.

Consider the following scenario. Your toddler is just under two years old and has started to take an interest in playing with the little potty you set up in the bathroom months ago. He wears it on his head, he fills it with little dinosaurs, he stands on top of it and dances. He uses it for everything, in fact, except for what it's there for. In an effort to help him get the gist of this object, your every toilet run has become an announced event.

"I think it's time I go pee-pee in the potty! Come along with me and watch!"

It doesn't matter what you're doing at the time. Watching TV, eating dinner, working in the garden. You tell the world about your impending bowel movement for the sole benefit of your child, who you really hope is listening and taking this all in.

You hope your toddler will follow you into the bathroom and sit on his potty, just like you're sitting on yours. And oftentimes they will, because there's nothing a toddler loves more than miniature versions of big people stuff. But too many times, that's all you can hope for.

Let's face it. Peeing and pooping is kind of complicated, when you really break it down for explanatory purposes. How do you describe bladder pressure? How do you describe the kind of feeling you get before you know it's time to sit on the toilet? Your toddler hasn't had to think about this kind of thing before. His diaper made sure of that. So you're left coming up with explanations that are more or less accurate, but radically simplified. "You make your water squirt out of your pee-pee." Or "Do you have a poop in your bum-bum?"

You can lead a tot to a potty, but you can't make him pee. That's the first big problem of potty training—getting them to realize which bodily functions they now need to deposit in the pot.

So you start watching for signs of pooping and peeing, and when you see it, you physically pick them up, take their diapers off, and sit them on the throne. Usually, the latter is easier to foretell than the former, since a lot of toddlers stop whatever they're doing and get a glazed look on their faces when about to poop. They also tend to use their whole bodies to push. Peeing is harder to predict, so you simply have them sit on the potty immediately after they've had their morning cup of juice.

And then you wait for something to come out. And wait. And wait.

Sometimes this can take years.

When and if your toddler does reward you with a little something in the pot, it's you who gets to make a huge stink, so to speak. You have to make sure your child knows he did the right thing and that you're very proud of him. Dance and sing. Call Grandma. Kiss him all over. The goal here is *reinforce the positive*! Feel free to ply him with candy, if you feel this will help ensure that he goes in the potty a second and third time.

And, of course, if he does start using the potty regularly, you're over the moon with pride. You'll regale all your friends and coworkers with every little detail of your child's latest bowel movement, whether or not they wanted to know. You'll tell everyone who didn't ask the whole potty training story, from first diaper to the latest all-cotton underwear. You'll spend your lunch pondering at length the relative merits of pull-ups versus training pants.

Why would anyone not going through the same thing want to hang out with you?

Hopefully, your toddler will start using the potty on some kind of a regular basis. It's fun for him to do big kid stuff, and he sees that it gets a good, possibly lucrative reaction out of you. But you're not out of the woods yet. Once you take the dramatic step of separating the toddler from his diaper (a very traumatic move in the eyes of some toddlers), you're really living life on the edge.

First, you have to buy the underwear. It has to be soft. Nonscratchy. And it has to have the right cartoon character on it. Some toddlers prefer underwear just like yours, in which case you'll have to scour Target and Kmart stores until you find children's underwear without any branding on it.

Then you have to start asking your toddler every fifteen minutes whether he has to go pee-pee. You want him to get used to the idea of telling you when he has to go, but you never trust him to do this before it's too late. It's all too common for your toddler to dutifully tell you he went pee-pee five minutes after the last time you asked. For this reason, you'll need a lot of paper towels and a washing machine.

If you're really brave, you'll venture on short trips with your underwear-clad toddler. But hopefully, you'll keep in close proximity to shops where you know there's a toilet you can use at the eleventh hour. Naturally, you'll have stuffed your diaper bag with four or five changes of clothing, as well as several diapers, in case he falls asleep in the car seat or stroller and all bladder/bowel control is off.

Potty Mouth

Since potty training is so, ah, earthy, you'll have to come up with a terminology for the details that suits your particular family. Bodily waste figures prominently in everyday household banter when you live with a toddler, so it's best to get over your sense of decorum. Euphemism is the name of the game here, and if you don't like talking about poo-poo and pee-pee, then you can safely hide behind words like BM (an abbreviation for *bowel movement*, for all you Victorians out there) for as long as you have small children in the house. Unfortunately, the product is somewhat easier to discreetly describe than the equipment. Lots of folks, at a complete loss for what to call their genitalia, and utterly loathe to use the formal nouns, revert happily back to whatever banalities their parents used with them. Your pee-pee and bum-bum. Your Willy. Your Mary Jane. Your little Peter. Your tushie. Your privates. You have to describe them in some manner. Just pick the most inoffensive.

At some point your toddler will start wearing underwear more often than not. And at some point, your toddler will start to use the potty as a matter of course. You might feel inclined to let down your guard. You might get cocky and leave the house without an extra pair of pants and an emergency cache of wipes. Don't.

There will be accidents. There are always accidents, and you can never ever predict what sets them off. Sometimes, a tot will be stressed out and let loose. Other times he'll be too

Of course, in this day and age, many parents insist on using only the proper terms, suggesting that cutesy euphemisms only make the child think there's something to hide down there. There is something to hide, in my mind. And that's your three-year-old dancing around the library singing "Vagina! Vagina! Vagina!" at the top of her lungs. Toddlers, especially the older variety, are always looking for new words to add to their burgeoning vocabularies, and they will delight in knowing the Latin terms for all that lies under their diapers. And the knowledge that what they possess differs from that of their siblings or friends of the opposite sex will fascinate them for weeks. You can hardly blame them for enthusiastically telling everyone they meet about their genitalia, much less showing them off. It's simply a matter of how comfortable you are discussing penises and vaginas with total strangers on the street.

busy to get to a potty in time. Sometimes, there's no reason at all. Yours is not to ask why; yours is only to be prepared. Staying dry all night is another matter. This often takes another year after potty training has been achieved. You'll just have to be patient.

Of course, like everything in parenting, it doesn't have to be this way. Some kids toilet-train themselves, and their parents are spared months of worry and gnashing of teeth over their effluvia. One twenty-monther in my courtyard is doing just that. "Nico just tells me when she's wet, and when she's not wearing a diaper she goes and puts it in the potty," shrugs my neighbor Mindy. "I've barely had to think about it."

Grrr. My daughter was just the opposite. We blithely followed the Brazelton method and didn't stress about it until she was well over two, and we began to wonder when she'd take an interest. As it turned out, Annie wasn't interested in going on the potty until she was three and a half years old, her baby brother had already been born, and I had been turned into a screaming maniac obsessed with not having to buy two different sizes of diapers. Of course, by this time there was no "training" involved, merely an agreement on her part to put her poop and pee where I wanted her to put it.

Toddlers are very literal-minded. They want to see what you've put into the toilet and how you put it there. Older toddlers will want to know why, and you'll have to tell them about eating food and how after your body uses what it needs, it flushes the rest of it out. Then you'll have to explain why what's in the potty doesn't look anything like what you had for breakfast that morning. Then they'll want to know why your genitalia doesn't look like theirs, or vice versa, and why Daddy pees standing up, and why Daddy brings a book to the potty and you don't. And so on and so on.

You'll have to get over your squeamishness very quickly if you want to potty-train successfully. Good luck.

Tools of the Trade

Here are the basics you'll need when it's potty-training time:

- **A potty.** Lots of different kinds to choose from. There are potty seats that go on top of the big toilet. There are little white plastic potties that sit on the floor, elaborate wooden potties with hand-painted flowers on the sides, simple plastic "pots" that a lot of kids seem to like. Pick something that your toddler won't scream and run away from.

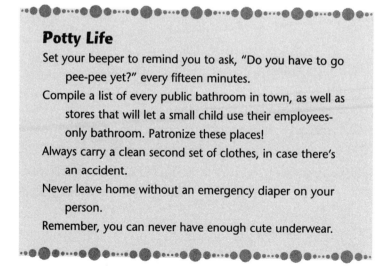

Potty Life

Set your beeper to remind you to ask, "Do you have to go pee-pee yet?" every fifteen minutes.

Compile a list of every public bathroom in town, as well as stores that will let a small child use their employees-only bathroom. Patronize these places!

Always carry a clean second set of clothes, in case there's an accident.

Never leave home without an emergency diaper on your person.

Remember, you can never have enough cute underwear.

- **A potty book.** If watching you and your mate go potty hasn't especially impressed junior, you might want to try a potty book. My favorite is Alona Frankel's *Once Upon a Potty*, which is wonderfully basic and, apart from strange pronoun usage, is aimed right at a toddler's sense of the literal.

- **A potty video.** More media influence. There are many out there. And kids this age can't seem to get enough of watching other kids do their thing. Again, my favorite is the Alona Frankel video version of her potty book. Catchy songs you'll sing at the office will alert your colleagues to your current preoccupation so they can avoid you.

- **Really cool underwear.** Call it a bribe if you must, but this is the underlying reason a lot of toddlers eventually potty-train themselves. Not only is it "big kid" underwear, but it comes with your kid's favorite cartoon character on it. And nobody wants to poop on Pikachu or Ariel, right?

Into the Bath

There are two kinds of toddlers in this world: those who love baths and those who hate them. Sometimes, they throw you off by acting like they hate bathing, only to revert to type when you try to get them out again. No matter what combination they throw at you, the end result is always the same: hassles galore at the end of the day.

Bathing is a subject toddlers have fierce views about. Of course, this is true about everything in a toddler's life, but bathing takes the biscuit because it involves a total loss of control on their part.

Think about it. First you're told that it's time to stop playing and take your clothes off. Then you're thrown into a tubful of water. Then—indignity of indignities—you're forcibly washed!

Bathtime is, for most households with toddlers, a decidedly unrelaxing time. Why this should be is especially perplexing to us adults, because to our minds, letting somebody else pour warm, fragrant water over us as we recline in the tub is just about the most luscious fantasy we can muster these days. Toddlers, however, don't know how good they have it.

Now, I have a confession to make. When my daughter was a baby, she got a bath once a week or less. I never understood some people's compunction to bathe their newborns every day. Sometimes I'd forget to bathe her for weeks at a time, unless she puked on herself or had one of those monster poops babies sometimes have that end up in their armpits. I'd wipe her face and hands down, sure, but there didn't seem to be much need for a full-on bath, since she didn't get that dirty and she didn't have any hair to speak of. This dramatically changed when she became a toddler. Most days she returns from day care covered with grass, dirt, and juice stains. (I take it as a sign she's had a great day.) I'm still not the biggest nut about cleanliness, but I do insist on at least three baths a week. This means we get to chase our daughter down and overpower her before she accepts her fate and soaks in the bathtub. Sometimes, she decides she doesn't want a bath and screams like we've taken an ax to her when we try to get her clothes off. This used to almost work, since she screamed and writhed so desperately we started to feel as if we were committing a violent crime and would stop.

But that was all part of her plan. By the time we finally saw through the ruse, realized that she wasn't afraid of anything, didn't have an illness, wasn't sunburned, or any other numerous reasons for trying to avoid bathtime, she smelled like a fifty-year-old barfly, and into the bath she went, screams and all. Now we don't give her a choice. It's bath or bust. Bathtime now falls under the "Because I said so and I'm the mommy" school of parenting.

Why do toddlers get so incredibly filthy? I have several theories.

First, there's the dirt ratio. The ratio of dirt to body proportion increases the older your toddler becomes. Once they've mastered the basics of mobility, a toddler takes it as his birthright to sample everything he comes into contact with. This includes mud, pet food, gravel, and the composting leaves at the foot of the driveway. It's no surprise, then, that the faster and more adroit they become, the wider the sample selection. Except that while they're that much more agile, they still can't seem to go a day without spilling things onto themselves, or falling into the mud, or wiping snot all over their faces.

If your toddler goes a day without spilling the contents of his cup, *call your doctor immediately!*

Then there is the exuberance factor. You no doubt have noticed the enthusiasm for living your toddler embraces. This enthusiasm informs his grime collecting over the course of the day. Ever watch a two-and-a-half-year-old eat a chocolate cupcake? Paint a picture on the wall? Invent ways to vex the cat? A toddler hasn't yet been socialized enough to think that there might be giant bugs under that rock, so he gleefully turns it over for inspection and gets gunk all over himself in the process. They're fearless when it comes to getting dirty.

Toddlers have a comfort level with dirt unknown to anyone over five. Maybe toddlers in the wild used a layer of dirt as warmth, but no toddler I've ever met seems to mind having a face full of schmutz. You're itching to get at their faces with a washcloth, and they'll pitch a fit if you get near them with one. It's just got to be written into the genetic code of tots. This goes for even those toddlers who are hyper-concerned with what's on their hands. It's one thing to have hands that are free from any adornment. It's quite another to go a day without fouling your face.

Here's a question for you: why will a toddler fight to the death to avoid being put into a warm, clean tub, but upon sighting a stagnant puddle in the middle of the park will run to sit in it as soon as you take your eyes off her for a second?

But I digress. After the dirt ratio and the exuberance factor, there's the psychology factor, which is the basic toddler belief that anything you want them to do must not be very much fun. Ergo washing hands, wiping mouths, or changing soiled clothes takes on all the allure of a doctor's visit. Trouble is, if you pretend not to notice how dirty they get, they'll happily go for months without a bath, and the neighbors are likely to call the authorities.

In the end, toddlers must be bathed!

So. Is it bathtime already?

To prepare yourself for bathtime means first preparing yourself for battle. Don the uniform—comfortable clothes that allow you to bend and contort as needed, and in fabric that dries quickly. I don't need to mention that whatever you wear should be colorfast.

Next, prepare the scene. Ignoring your child's screams that he doesn't want a bath, fill the bathtub anyway. Employ whatever seductive toys you have that will lure him closer to the tub. Have the no-tear shampoo and the Elmo soap at the ready. Don't forget the all-important cup and washcloth for when it's the dreaded hair-washing time.

Finally, get the kid into the tub.

How you do it depends on your toddler's temperament, your patience level, and your tolerance for getting soaked to the bone. At our house, we've perfected the art of bath giving through a crafty series of toddler initiatives. Try these yourself.

- **Seduction.** We found a set of foam mommy and baby animals that stick to the side of the tub. I draw a bath, and as Annie is screaming that she doesn't want a bath, I set these animals enticingly on the ledge of the tub. It always works. She's always lured in. Little tablets that turn the water blue, or purple, or green. A toy shark. A Little Mermaid doll. The toy manufacturers of America, God bless them, have something out there that will entice your toddler into the bathtub. Find it. Buy it. Use it.

• **Bribery.** "If we have a quick bath right now, you'll be able to watch this new video I bought you." Substitute whatever treat your toddler is obsessing about this week: ice cream, Happy Meals, pirate stories. Don't ever be ashamed to use what works! Just make sure you follow through—a toddler never forgets, and if you try to fudge it, you're asking for a Force Three tantrum for sure.

• **The fear of God.** Make your toddler understand that the Great, All-Knowing, All-Seeing Mommy will frown deeply if she doth protest too much. If you can somehow get it across that you're serious and you won't be put off, this will be the bottom line your toddler will eventually cow to. Please notice I said *eventually.*

Once a toddler has admitted defeat and agreed to get into the bath, you can enjoy a few moments of rest while he enjoys himself in this new watery wonderworld. Unfortunately, at some point you actually have to start bathing him.

Parents worldwide agree: shampooing a toddler's hair is the most dreaded chore on the list of hygienic necessities. No toddler in his right mind willingly submits to this most horrible of tortures, and it's always a fight—a soggy, slippery fight to the death. Or at least to the final rinse.

To successfully wash your toddler's hair, you have to again resort to many of the same methods you used to get him into the bath in the first place. You might have to rattle that giant shampoo bottle shaped like Elmo in front of him, give him the washcloth with the baby chicks on it to cover his face with, and rinse with the big shark cup you got from 7-Eleven. Or maybe even these things won't work, and you'll have to resort to your superior strength and fleetness.

Later, of course, you'll have to brush out his hair. The moms in my courtyard all agree that the many hair detangling sprays now on the market are a godsend—providing the toddler stands still long enough for you to dry, spray, then comb out those knotty snarls in the first place. Then there's drying it . . . but you get the picture. We don't need to go there just yet.

Toddler Hairstyles

Toddler hair can, when clean and brushed and cut right, put any shampoo ad model to shame. It glows with youth. Both the sun and the moon bounce off it. It curls into the most perfect innocent little tendrils around their sleeping faces, and no matter how dirty it gets, it always looks cute. As my stepmother, a hairdresser for thirty years, once commented, "We'd have to pay $200 for highlights like that."

Most toddler hair I've come into contact with, however, doesn't live up to its potential. For most toddlers, standing still and allowing you to brush their hair is simply anathema to everything they believe in. You can try arguing. You can try to chase them down. In the end, you're beaten down into apathy, and you stop caring what their hair looks like unless you're taking them to Grandma's, at which point the hunt must begin anew.

We've all seen toddlers with gorgeous locks—really long, beautiful manes of hair. I'm told that some tots, boys as well as girls, really get into the idea of hair care. And this seems to be the only caveat to toddlers and their general hatred of being fussed over. It seems once the toddler him or herself has decided that they want pretty hair with little baubles woven into it, they'll agree to a certain amount of parental primping to achieve the desired look.

Of course, nobody gets to choose the kind of toddler we have. Yours might be the ultimate in girly girls (even your boy might fall into this category), or you have the other model— the kind for whom hair is merely another body part to rub dirt and food into.

My daughter has beautiful, straight, dark blonde hair that strongly resembles spun gold when brushed. Problem is, she won't let me get near her with a brush, ever. I'll chase her

Practical Toddler Haircuts

Crew Cut—Nothing says "discipline" like a crew cut. Of course, it may also scream, "Yes, I lost the battle and chopped her hair off instead, thank you."

Pageboy—Unisex and universally cute. The kind of cut barbers and the hacks at the children's specialty salons can do on a writhing toddler in under five minutes.

Dreadlocks—Solves the brushing problem and looks very hip as well. Might not go over too well in suburban, rural, or overly white neighborhoods, though.

through the apartment until she's cowering behind a stool in the kitchen with her head between her legs, or until she crawls under the couch where I can't reach her, at which point she knows I'm apt to give up. I've tried all manner of ways to entice her into appreciating her beautiful hair—butterfly clips, fancy barrettes, headbands with glitter, ribbons. Absolutely nothing works. I've often wondered how long it would take to coax her snarls into dreadlocks, because not only would they be easier to deal with, they'd be way cool to boot (although Grandma would have a heart attack). In the end, I've opted for the short pageboy cut, which is not only cute, but also easy to care for, with the added bonus of being acceptable to all relatives over the age of forty-five.

After the washing of the hair comes the much easier washing of the extremities. After that, your duties as official hygienist are through, and you're free to sit nearby and read the Pottery Barn catalog while your toddler enthusiastically entertains himself in the water. This reprieve is brief, however. Within the hour the bath is going tepid, the soap suds are gone, and your toddler is pruning up. Time to start Bathtime: Phase II.

Bedtime: The Final Battle

After all that mental and physical energy spent getting your tot into the bath and washed up, you now have two more putsches to execute before you're home free for the night. But these two are doozies. It's terrifically unfair of the cosmos to put these two tasks at the very end of the day, but what can you do?

You have to get your toddler out of the bath.

You have to get your toddler into bed.

Now, the common wisdom is that after a nice, warm bath, a little kid should be mellowed out and getting sleepy. I suppose this could be true, although no toddler worth his salt will admit to that condition.

Toddlers do not like to admit defeat. As such, they rarely agree to go to bed on their own. Even as they're swaying as they stand and rubbing their poor little red eyes every half minute, they're loudly insisting that THEY ARE NOT TIRED! You obviously know by now to take your cues from the physical, never the verbal, when toddlers are concerned.

At this point, he knows and you know that his time is nigh. The threshold between slumber and Force Three tantrum is thin. You must move swiftly to complete the bedtime ritual.

Step One: Tell him that bathtime is over in five minutes. Put the sharks away. Make the last pot of "tea." He'll ignore you, but at least you can say you gave him his due diligence.

Step Two: Tell him bathtime is officially over. He'll ignore you louder.

Step Three: You have a choice—either pick him up out of the tub (which can get messy) or do as I do and simply drain the tub. Toddlers are a stubborn lot, but I've never heard of one yet who'll stay longer than a few minutes shivering on the cold porcelain of an empty bathtub.

Step Four: Wrap him up and snuggle for a bit.

Step Five: Brush out his hair and put on his pajamas.

You'll note I'm glossing over these last two, which can be traumas unto themselves. But I do so because what you're really interested in here is the supreme battle, by which I mean GETTING THE TODDLER INTO BED.

I have heard tales of the occasional toddler asking to be put to bed. My own daughter did it once, which shocked us into silence. If they're not pretending to play "bedtime," this can usually mean only one thing: the toddlers in question are coming down with something, and know it. If this is the case, by all means make them warm and cozy and give them kisses and backrubs until they're asleep and then hover over them all night and ignore the following paragraphs.

An otherwise normal, healthy toddler views bedtime as an extreme sport, and he's prepared to enjoy it fully. For some unknown reason, small children tend to wind themselves up for a final putsch just as your own inner resources are dwindling, making the bedtime battle particularly grueling. "I spend so much energy getting him into bed that I'm exhausted by the end of it," my friend Alex told me recently. "His bedtime is now my bedtime, for all intents and purposes, because I'm too tired to do anything afterward."

A quiet toddler will become loud. An aggressive toddler will start throwing things. An active toddler will start running laps around the house. It's almost like they know what's coming up, so they're consciously dumping extra fuel, like airplanes coming in for crash landings. This energy level naturally makes it hard to get their pajamas on, much less their hair combed out and dry. Try sitting on them.

Then you have to brush their teeth. Sigh.

Hopefully, you've learned by now that toddlers respond well to both bribes and marketing. Hopefully, you've bought your toddler a really keen toothbrush of her very own, with her favorite cartoon character on it. Maybe this is all you had to do to get your toddler to brush her teeth. But probably not.

Getting a toddler to brush and brush decently takes a detailed and individualized plan. Parents of toddlers I know have described a variety of tricks and incentives they've used, to mixed results. One mom told her son that there was a monster in his mouth and his Elmo toothbrush had to brush it away. "It worked for a few weeks, anyway," she says. Another pits his two children against each other, in the understanding that competition breeds excellence. He gives small prizes to whomever brushes their teeth best (and alternates them every night). Most of the time, however, getting your child to brush his teeth well means you have to do it for him. And in the interest of expediency, why the hell not?

Your toddler is bathed and jammied. His hands are clean (for the time being) and his teeth are brushed. Now what?

Remember the golden toddler rules of discipline and consistency? Nowhere do these two words become more important than during the bedtime hour. If you can establish a routine that works for both you and the toddler, and by that I mean a plan that is a perfect blend of compromise and firmness, then you can survive this nightly ordeal, uh, nightly.

Your objective: get your toddler into bed so you can watch thirty minutes of TV in peace and quiet before falling asleep yourselves.

Toddler's objective: stay awake and keep parents interacting with you for as long as possible before sleep sneaks up and snatches you for the night.

Compromise: everyone passes out by 10 P.M.

Figure out a decent hour for bedtime and stick to it. Create a best-case-scenario schedule (bedtime at 8, kid down by 8:30) as well as a more realistic schedule you can at least live with (bedtime at 8, kid down by 9:20). At least try to get your bedtime routine started by your stated bedtime. That way junior knows the jig is up when you call the hour, and the games can begin.

Create a routine. You've got to calm your toddler down while getting him ready for sleep. So give him incentives for going along with the diaper changes or the potty visits and the final indignity of bed. A short video often does the trick, as does reading his latest favorite book (again) or singing his favorite song. Have a snuggle or rub his back. If he knows he can expect these creature comforts every night, he'll go a little more willingly into that fair good night.

Establish rules. Only two books. Only one, OK, maybe two, sips of water. You might waffle on the number of kisses (who can resist?), but you're firm on only one monster inspection. Don't fall for the potty trap, either. If you're a lenient sort, you can also establish physical boundaries in lieu of an actual bedtime. After our standard bedtime routine, we often let Annie read a book with the hall light on, as long as she stays in bed. She has (correctly) interpreted this to mean that as long as she stays in her bedroom with the lights off and plays quietly (i.e., she doesn't come out and bug us anymore), we won't object.

Know where the line is. Your toddler will naturally push you on the bedtime thing. Make sure he knows there's an hour when you'll stop being nice about it. I'll give my daughter until 10:30 before I start yelling and ignoring her pleas for another drink of water. Your hour may vary.

Your reward will come sometime after your toddler has departed for la-la land, and you get to sneak in and look at him sleeping, all pink-cheeked and perfect, clutching his little bear. You'll feel like very successful parents, and your love for him will gush all over the room. Enjoy it, because you won't feel this way in the morning when it's time to get him up and dressed and the battle begins anew.

Fashionistas

There is a little girl in our courtyard for whom dressing up isn't merely a cute pastime: it is a way of life. This toddler—I'll call her Claudia—has an array of fabulous, sequined outfits that would make a drag queen sick with envy. Every day she arrives on the scene in a different ensemble. Sometimes she is Snow White. Other days she is a butterfly, or a ballerina, or a medieval princess. "She even dresses for dinner," her mom Jane tells me. "With gloves and matching shoes and everything."

Toddler parents agree that dressing up becomes a favorite toddler pastime sometime after the imagination has kicked in at around eighteen months and escalates until at least kinder-garten, when peer pressure compels them to leave their Spiderman costume at home. It starts when a toddler figures out how to open drawers and pull out whatever clothing items are inside. At some point they learn how to undress themselves, usually by age two (getting naked is also a favorite toddler exercise, but more on that later), and the idea of putting on other clothes occurs to them. Their dressing up charades become more elaborate the more able they become to dress themselves. For this reason, younger toddlers favor hats, which are easy to put on, and scarves and jewelry, while older toddlers like whole ensembles.

Toddlers don't distinguish between actual costumes and fashion creations of their own design. By two and a half many toddlers insist on choosing their own clothes for the day, however inappropriate, and you have no choice but to let them. Where do they get their fashion sense? Nobody knows. But if you try to squelch them, you'll suffer for it. My advice is to just adapt. My neighbor Stafford's daughter used to insist on wearing two different shoes to day care each morning. "I finally just started slipping her the right and left shoe from two different pairs so at least they fit properly," he says. Last summer my daughter took to wearing her bathing suit over her clothes, with rainboots to clinch the look. All I could do was smooth out the wrinkles and let her strut.

Gender makes no difference. Even though experts say gender identification usually starts manifesting itself at around three, it's true that there are girly girls and manly boys well before that, as well as vice versa. Still, no three-year-old boy in the world will say no to a cape and a pair of boots, no matter how butch he is. As I write this, every boy under five in our courtyard sports a superhero cape left over from Halloween. Other boys beg to wear their sister's tutu. You can't (and shouldn't) discriminate on what costume you

Das Boot

Never underestimate the power of the common boot to the toddler set. My neighbor Peter's twenty-month-old daughter, Nicola, is seriously into boots. The other day she put on her own rainboots to go downstairs and play in the puddles. No sooner had she gotten downstairs than she saw Lulu's new rainboots outside her door and had to wear those, "for only a minute," she told her dad. So he put those on her. In the courtyard they met up with me and my daughter. Annie had on her red sparkly shoes, a highly coveted commodity in themselves, but was carrying her Teletubbie boots. Nicola went for those, but Annie, being three and a half, snatched them up with a loud declaration of ownership. Then Lulu, seventeen months, came outside and saw that her new blue rainboots were being worn by another toddler. To make matters worse, several four-year-olds then ran by, each in their own big-kid boots, headed for fun in the mud. Pandemonium ensued until we got everybody wearing their own boots and let them loose in the puddles, which is where they all wanted to be anyway. The lesson here? Better to lose your wallet than your toddler's rainboots.

let your toddler wear, because a tot in costume is a happy, nonscreaming tot.

Besides, all the world smiles upon a toddler in drag, anyway. It's one of the more charming character traits of a toddler: their insistence on wearing their own fashion creations as they go about their normal day. I think it must have something to do with getting public validation that, yes, in fact, they *are* the center of the universe. My daughter has a pink velvet and tulle "princess" dress that she wears all over, and everyone from the clerk at the store to the bum on the street corner comments favorably on it. Annie just beams like royalty. A toddler parent friend once remarked that it must be wonderful to be the age where nobody looks at you strangely for going about town in a green hula skirt and red cowboy boots. I must concur.

While this penchant for dressing up is universally regarded as harmless, parents of toddlers do have to contend with a certain practical element. Even as your son insists on sleeping in his Batman cape, he will also insist on wearing it outside in March during an ice storm. It's a real trick to convince a toddler *en ensemble* that he has to cover his look with a dreadfully boring coat. One trick is to get a warm wrap that is as close to a costume as possible. People actually used to wear capes for warmth, so why can't BabyGap sell a functional little Red Riding Hood cape? Betcha it would sell billions.

You also have to convince your toddler that getting out of costume periodically, usually for bed, is a good thing. This is usually accomplished by buying really cool pajamas that look like Batman's outfit, for example, or a dalmatian suit, or a frilly Victorian nightgown. You're trading one costume for another, sure, but at least it gives you a chance to launder the day suit. In the end, there's little you can do to get your toddler back into normal clothes until his fantasy has played out. The good news is, everyone who's ever had a toddler will

Toddler Fashion Accessories

Boots—Nothing makes a toddler happier than his own pair of boots. These can be rainboots, cowboy boots, hiking boots, or go-go boots: the common denominator being they are different than shoes, and you pull them on. They make toddlers impervious to puddles and very dramatic to boot.

Sparkly shoes—Lots of discount stores like Target and KMart sell these shoes, which are really just Mary Janes but covered in glitter. Every two-to-three-year-old girl on the planet wants a pair of sparkly shoes.

Cape—Since they're going to make one using a baby blanket anyway, you might as well cave and buy or make them a cheap cape for all their fantasy needs.

Umbrellas—A fashion accessory no toddler can live without. Fair weather is never an excuse.

Hats—Almost any hat will do, but it's always better to give your toddler a hat he has already seen you wearing.

Long beads—At some point, toymakers wised up and started creating long strands of sturdy, nonchokable plastic beads for the toddler set, to the eternal gratitude of mothers everywhere, who could now take their real jewelry out of hiding.

smile warmly and forgive you any fashion faux pas. Day-care and preschool workers are used to greeting kids in all manner of getups each morning, including those still in their pajamas, and so are unlikely to give you grief, either. In the end, toddlers and their fashions are one of those battles that is a non-battle. Just relax, keep your sense of humor about you, and take a lot of pictures.

Travel Alert

There should be an international law banning travel with toddlers between the ages of two and three. I say this as a parent who has had to travel myself with a toddler, and as a person who's been forced to sit next to a parent traveling with a toddler. I can't say which situation is more hellacious.

As parents of toddlers, you need to constantly remind yourself that it's not in your best interest to go anywhere during this time. Even the common car trip, if it lasts more than forty minutes, can turn a pleasant day into a traumatic experience for everyone involved. There are lots of reasons for this.

For starters, unlike you, toddlers are not interested in breaking up the monotony of their lives. You may be chomping at the bit to get away from the grinding sameness of parenthood, but your kids thrive on that very grinding sameness. At an age where most of what they want to do is beyond their ability to pull off, toddlers take great comfort in routine and repetition. This explains the multiple viewings of Teletubbie videos, but it also explains why they tend to implode when taken out of their own environments.

This is as true for the tame trip to Disneyland, which is geared toward small children, as it is for more exotic travels. I always chuckle when I read accounts of people who had the brilliant idea of taking an overseas trip with their small children in tow. "We didn't see why having children should stop us from having adventures," they write. Obviously, they pen sentences like these before they've had their children. Instead of conjuring up images of exotic locales, articles like these make me wonder how these foolish parents deal with the typical toddler attitude on the road. What happens to naps? You think a toddler will eat food from an Indian street vendor when she won't even finish her plate of known food at home? Do you *want* her eating from a street vendor? And if not, are you planning on smuggling a year's supply of frozen fish sticks into the third world? Do you realize what happens when toddlers get tired and hungry at the same time? What happens when this toddler refuses to walk anymore and lies face down on the sidewalk, or the dirt road, as the case may be? How about when she wants to go in the opposite direction you need to go and starts screaming in protest? How do you carry your stuff on your back and the toddler's stuff? What happens when you lose her special dolly or his favorite blanket, God forbid? The list of questions grows in my mind until I'm forced to the obvious conclusion: *why would any sane person take their toddler traveling anywhere?*

By the time your kids are old enough to want to go exploring the world, they certainly don't want to explore it with you. And you've moved on to the Club Med Golfing Extravaganza vacation package, anyway. It's a gruesome catch-22, but there it is.

How to Travel with a Toddler

First, ask yourself if you really must take this trip. If it can't be avoided, take a deep breath and prepare for the absolute worst. Having no expectations often makes the trip more pleasant.

Our first trip to England to visit in-laws was so bad it was a full year before I agreed to even think about a second trip. Annie was thirteen months and just walking. She'd also just had her dreaded MMR (measles/mumps/rubella) shot the day before. This brings us to the First Rule of Toddler Travel:

Always assume your toddler will get violently ill the night before a big trip. It is prudent to calculate this into your schedule. And pack appropriately.

Packing extra clothes, even for a child who is allegedly potty-trained, is very wise. The second time we went to England, Annie slipped and fell into a puddle of another toddler's pee at the airport play area. Our bags were already checked, and I had to drop $30 for a dress with the Golden Gate Bridge on it at the airport tourist shop, which Annie ultimately refused to wear, anyway. Thus, the Second Rule of Toddler Travel:

Pack an essential toddler bag containing everything you could possibly need for your child, including several changes of clothes, favorite foods, favorite blanket, and favorite toy. Bring new toys your child hasn't seen for especially long trips.

Travel Conundrums

Your days of throwing a few things into a backpack and taking off are over for good. Here are a few of the more perplexing dilemmas of traveling with your toddler.

- **Car seat.** It's heavy, it's awkward, and it's going to take twenty minutes to strap into the airport shuttle, irritating the driver, who probably doesn't like kids, anyway, not to mention the other passengers, all of whom are running late. People in foreign countries are nowhere near as strict as we are about car seats (but hey, all their children have full medical coverage) and are likely to view you as an irritating rich American if you insist on putting yours into every taxi you get into. But you've seen how those taxi drivers drive. Do you schlepp the car seat or not?

- **Fast food.** You're in France. Or Italy, or somewhere else where the local cuisine is the reason for being there. But your toddler refuses to eat any of it. Then you spy a McDonald's. What do you do?

- **Far-flung relatives.** They're desperate to see the latest family addition. But you'll have to travel almost twenty hours to see them, and when you do, your child will be traumatized by all the strangers pinching her cheeks. Do you go or do you just send a video?

- **Sightseeing.** You used to travel in part to see the world and its treasures. Big Ben! The Louvre! The Grand Canyon! Your toddler won't be impressed by any of it and will agitate all day to return to the market on main street with the tacky little merry-go-round outside next to the cigarette machines. Do you do your sightseeing in shifts, or do you take him along and ignore his whining?

Isn't socialization fun? It makes dealing with a colicky four-month-old seem like, pardon the expression, child's play. But it's all part of your job, and you'll enjoy the fruits of your labor sometime down the line when your child gets up to be at school every weekday morning at 8:30 with his homework done and his hair washed, and he almost makes it by himself.

Now can you see why people without kids look ten years younger than we do?

4

TALES FROM DAY CARE

"Where there's a will, there's a way.
And where there's a child, there's a will."
—Marceline Cox, *Ladies Home Journal* (1950)

Well, here you are. Standing at the entrance to that dark, dank cave known as the Terrible Twos. It's scary. You don't want to go in, but you don't have much of a choice. There are a lot of parents who will tell you that Terrible Twos, like the month of March, come in like a lion and go out like a lamb. This wasn't my experience at all. My daughter entered the Twos like a lamb and then came out like a lion. And I know plenty of other parents for whom the

Terrible Twos come in like a lion and go out like a bigger, meaner lion. So there's no point in listening to the stereotypes in this case. Just put your head down, take a deep breath, and enter the dragon.

Portrait of a Two-Year-Old

Like most stereotypes, the Terrible Twos is based mostly in reality. I say mostly, because not every two-year-old is a screaming, unmanageable tyrant (most two-and-a-half-year-olds are, however). Some parents I've met insist on referring to this year as the "terrific twos," which is fine if you like to put a sugar coating on everything, but the truth is, two-year-olds do have a certain *je ne sais quoi* about them. For the first time, there's more child there than baby. Many two-year-olds are talking in full, more or less understandable, sentences. They're curious about everything around them, and while they're getting into everything, they're being damned cute about it. You'll find them sleeping in the bottom of your computer box or singing a garbled version of the ABCs song at the top of their lungs in the library, and you can hardly be mad at them. They're also much more social beings than ever before. They seek out the company of other kids, even though social skills like sharing and not hitting are still beyond them.

There's a slight downside to all this socialization, though. You can keep your child as "pure" as you want him, knowing only the sound of your voice reading him the classics, tasting only the most expensive organic fruits and vegetables, only as long as he's home full time with you. When you launch him into the greater world, either now or in a few years when kindergarten starts, it's all over. He'll meet the beast. And within a week, he'll be demanding Twinkies and a Dragon Tales T-shirt.

Happy Meals, Disney products, toy guns, Beanie Babies, Barbie. All that is questionable about American culture is lying in wait for your toddler. It's waiting to turn him or her into a proper little first world capitalist.

And it all starts in day care.

The Day-Care Affair

Until fairly recently, children born on Israeli kibbutzim slept not with their parents, but in children's houses. One supposes this was to reinforce the idea of the group over the individual and to get the kids used to the idea of having to share their piece of the pie with others in the community. It doesn't seem like such a bad idea to me, this notion of community—since all you have to do is watch a toddler light up when other kids come into the room to see that most of us are hardwired for company. But for years now, Americans have liked their homes single-family and private, and the idea of raising a child at home in isolation has somehow become the ideal we're all supposed to want. I think most everyone agrees that there's little to be served by putting a six-week-old into day care full time unless there's just no alternative. But I think (and I believe the experts back me up on this) that by the time that baby is approaching two, he's ready for some outside socialization. Let's face it, two years is a long time to spend with anybody day in and day out. Your tot naturally wants to broaden his social circle outside the nest.

A good day-care situation is a boon for everyone involved.

How do you define "good" day care? State regulators have their own definition, but I define good day care as a clean, warm place where the ratio of kids to teachers isn't too alarming; where there are lots of age-appropriate toys, several nutritious meals a day, a warm, caring provider who you get a good vibe from, and an easygoing, toddler-friendly schedule.

It's also optimum to find a place where the spread of ages isn't too great. Although toddlers thrill to be in the company of older kids, a lone tot in a room full of seven-year-olds is going to be one bored, frustrated toddler. Likewise if the day care has too many infants around. All toddlers love infants, but infants can't interact with them as they'd like, and infants

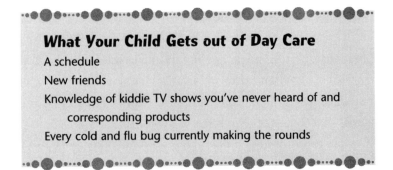

What Your Child Gets out of Day Care

A schedule

New friends

Knowledge of kiddie TV shows you've never heard of and
corresponding products

Every cold and flu bug currently making the rounds

tend to monopolize the caregiver's time. Better to look for a place where there are four or five kids within a three-year span of each other. That way they'll have playmates and peers at the same time.

Not only do toddlers get a lot out of a good day-care situation, parents get a lot out of it, too. Dare I say it—we might even get more out of it, mostly because we appreciate what we're getting.

Day care can provide you with a delirious sense of freedom, the likes of which you haven't tasted since before you were a parent. Imagine. A whole day without your toddler underfoot! If you went back to work at an earlier junction, then you're already well-acquainted with this delicious feeling of freedom. But if you've stayed home with your kid thus far, a few days of day care are almost more than you can handle, since you've now acclimated to dealing with simple chores while accompanied by an irrational, hair-trigger personality. It's like suddenly pulling an empty cart when you're used to pulling one with a 100-pound barbell inside. You're too efficient for your own good. Once you've dropped your toddler off for the day, you're apt to do the shopping, visit the

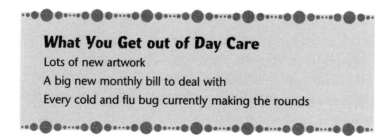

What You Get out of Day Care

Lots of new artwork

A big new monthly bill to deal with

Every cold and flu bug currently making the rounds

post office, clean the house, wash the car, pay the bills, weed the garden, and start dinner all before 2 P.M. Now what? The possibilities boggle the mind.

Sometimes stay-at-home moms I have known feel guilty for putting their toddlers into day care for part or all of the day. They're home, after all. Shouldn't they be taking care of their own children?

Pish, I say. By age two, you deserve a break, and so does your toddler. Maybe this is a juicy rationalization on my part, but I think a good day-care situation is almost the best thing for a toddler. In a good day care, your toddler enjoys the company of his peers, and with them, a regular and reliable

The Five Kinds of Day-Care Kids

- **The ADD kid.** The boy who vexes your day-care provider and prevents her from giving her fair share of attention to the rest of the group.
- **The girly girl.** The girl with the bows in her hair. And the Barbie accessories. And the fancy dresses every day.
- **The bully.** This boy or girl bites. They hit. They take your kid's cookie, and they pitch a tantrum if foiled by the day-care provider.
- **The best friend.** The one your child talks about incessantly. The one your child wants to go home with instead of you.
- **The crybaby.** Crying when you get there, crying when you return in the evening, this kid never seems to adapt to life in a group.

routine, probably including some outside time, a hot lunch, regular snacks, and an enforced nap. He also learns social skills he has no motivation to learn when he's at home with you. These include cleaning up, not pushing, not biting, attempting to share, and how to hold on to a leash and walk obediently in a group en route to the park. Sometimes, you even get a little schooling in there, too.

Day cares come in many different packages. Finding any of them requires a lot of research, much word of mouth, and a strong dose of luck. What you ultimately choose depends on your finances, your work situation, your child's temperament, and what's at hand when you need it most. Here are a few of the most common.

Day-Care Center

These tend to be allied with larger institutions like universities or really progressive workplaces. The upside is that they're often subsidized if you're also attached to the same institution, and they usually give first preference to you. Teachers and other staff might also be subsidized, so the 100 percent turnover that plagues the rest of the day-care world doesn't apply here. The downside? They're big, impersonal places that may smack of a warehouse more than anything else. You have no idea if the teacher even remembers your child's name, much less give her any kind of individualized attention. A rigid routine is the only way to manage such a large group of kids, and your child is forced to learn how to fend for herself or fall through the cracks. Some toddlers, however, adapt very well and learn how to capture the lion's share of attention for themselves. This is both good and bad when she returns to the home front.

Family Day Care
In which a toddler goes to a woman's home (and it's pretty much always a woman) and stays the day with a small group of other kids. The upsides include being in a small group environment in a comfortable home setting. You can usually find a woman who's been providing day care for years and is very good with children. Your child will get the benefit of hot, home-cooked meals and will be able to bond closely with the other kids there, even if they're not particularly close in age. But what happens when your day-care lady gets sick, or has to go out of town for an emergency, or any one of a

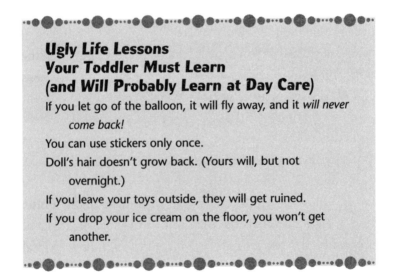

**Ugly Life Lessons
Your Toddler Must Learn
(and Will Probably Learn at Day Care)**

If you let go of the balloon, it will fly away, and it *will never come back!*

You can use stickers only once.

Doll's hair doesn't grow back. (Yours will, but not overnight.)

If you leave your toys outside, they will get ruined.

If you drop your ice cream on the floor, you won't get another.

number of situations that come up in day-to-day life? If you think she's inconvenienced by jury duty, what about you?

Nanny Share

Many families hire a nanny to watch two or more kids at a designated house, which can be a more affordable version of the nanny option. A toddler can become close to the nanny while enjoying a home setting and the company of one or two other toddlers. The downside I've seen is that when you get two or three families who want to go the nanny route, a change of circumstance in any one of them means change for everyone. One family moves, one family decides it doesn't like the nanny, the nanny can't work with one of the children, one child starts preschool—the potential for change is actually very high. This means there is more flux than what the arrangement originally suggests. Vacation time can get complicated as well. Do you pay the nanny for your two weeks of vacation, even if you're not using her services? If not, then the other family in your arrangement won't want to, either, and chances are you won't have your nanny very long.

Tantrum Management

Having a toddler is a lot like having fireworks in the house: you do everything you can to keep them from going off, but inevitably they always will, and it's you who'll have to deal with the consequences.

Tantrums go with toddlers like cookies go with milk and Ernie goes with Bert. They're as sure as death and taxes—and about as pleasant. You can't avoid them if you have a small child, but you can learn what causes them, if only so you don't waste precious brain cells blaming yourself. You can also learn the details of what sets off your particular toddler, so you can do your best to avoid them as you go about your day. This makes your day a lot like strolling through a minefield.

Long before you were a parent, your intimate knowledge of tantrums was probably quite sketchy. No doubt you'd watch a tantrum unfold from two rows back on the airplane and groan. You'd chalk it up to bad character on the part of the child or gross incompetence on the part of the parents; either way, you viewed it as a character flaw that could otherwise be avoided.

You're about to learn better.

Tantrums, by themselves, have nothing to do with a child's character. Sure, some toddlers can throw longer, louder, more violent tantrums than others, but this is more a matter of personality. Some people are just more cranky or high strung than others. Nor do tantrums have anything to do with your parenting skills. Child psychologists have toddlers who throw tantrums. Pediatricians have toddlers who tantrum. Even candy store owners have toddlers who tantrum. Toddlers will tantrum no matter what. You can't do anything about it.

Except that you can sometimes. You can cut down on your daily tantrum throwing by at least 40 percent if you know how to read the signs that she's about to blow. Think of your toddler as an anthropological field study. You need to observe her closely in her native environment and watch her feeding and grooming habits for trigger points. What time does she wake in the morning, and what kind of mood is she likely to be in? What happens if her favorite bowl isn't washed? Will she eat an egg or will she only accept Fruity Pebbles? What's she like if you keep her inside all day? What happens if she doesn't get a cookie in the afternoon? Does she hate it when the sun gets in her eyes on the drive home? By avoiding the situations you know will set your toddler off, you can be prepared—with a food offering, a diversion, a bribe, a pair of Barbie sunglasses. It's a lot like stepping on eggshells, but you'll be a saner parent in the end.

Unfortunately, there are a certain number of tantrums that can't be avoided. Toddlers worldwide teeter on the edge when they're either tired or hungry or, God forbid, both. You can't fault them for this. You can only be prepared. Since a toddler can be tired and/or hungry in the morning, afternoon, and evening, the golden rule of tantrum management is this: always have a snack on hand, no matter where you are. There's not a lot a juice box and a little baggie of raisins won't help cure. For a few moments, anyway.

Unavoidable though they are, tantrums also come in several flavors. You, as the parent of a toddler, need to become aware of the major genus of tantrums to know how best to handle each one.

Force One
Public Embarrassment Factor: 3.5 (on a scale of 1–10)

A Force One tantrum, also known as your simple meltdown, can be unpleasant, but for the most part, you expect it, and it doesn't do any serious damage. You told your toddler no candy before dinner (or no to the third cupcake), and so the crying begins. Force One tantrums are often more like full-throttle whining than actual crying. They are usually the result of weariness and are often precipitated by a transition, such as being picked up from day care or leaving a play date. There's not anything you can do to nip them in the bud, since they're mostly just the toddler's version of a Scotch on the rocks to unwind at the end of the day. But you can ease the transition a bit by offering a little snack to take the edge off. I know, again with the snacks. But they work!

Force Two
Public Embarrassment Factor: 6

A bit more alarming than a Force One. A Force Two tantrum often involves some kind of biting or hitting, or at the very mildest, some flailing about on the floor. There may be some prolonged screaming, some stomping, maybe even some throwing of toys. You must react very carefully with a Force Two tantrum. If you say the wrong thing, it could blow up into a Force Three before your very eyes. And since you really don't know what sort of utterance might be wrong— "Sweetheart, do you want a hug?" might very well send them over the edge—it's usually better to say nothing at all. Force Two tantrums are fairly upsetting, but if you let them run their course, they will usually blow over before thirty minutes are over.

Force Three
Public Embarrassment Factor: 15
Remember *The Exorcist*?

This is that kind of tantrum. It's a core meltdown. It's werewolf time. These are the full-body tantrums that leave you watching in astonishment as your toddler thrashes and screams and/or turns unique shades of blue. These are the kind of tantrums in which you start to wonder if your kid is still a human, and there's nothing you can do to mitigate it. The best thing you can do is make sure she's safe in her room, with nothing to pull down on top of herself, and let her have it out by herself. Most times a toddler will run down and either fall asleep or agree to let you into the room for a long, calming hug. But be prepared to wait for this moment for up to an hour.

Handling tantrums at home is relatively a piece of cake. If you can clear a space in her room and get her there, you can be fairly certain your toddler will live to tantrum another day. You can even shut the door and walk away while the tantrum runs its course. It's a lot like doing the laundry.

Unfortunately, you have to go out in public sometimes, and toddlers seem to know that the persuasion value of a tantrum is tripled if that tantrum is thrown in front of an audience.

Anywhere there's a floor to spread out on is a likely place for a tantrum, but for some reasons, toddlers like a venue with maximum tension potential. Busy parking lots are popular for this reason. Same with street corners off major thoroughfares. And don't ever forget the number-one all-time most popular place to throw a Force Three tantrum: airplanes.

People without kids never seem to realize how far we'll go to stave off a public display of screaming on the part of our toddlers. Do they think we enjoy standing over a hissing, flailing creature of our own creation? Do they think we just tune it out like we tune out the standard everyday whining? Don't they ever see us whispering frantically into our children's ears, "OK, OK, I'll get you the Pop Rocks, just don't start screaming. . . ."

Of course they don't. And so while we stand there, a bag of groceries in either hand and a bladder so full it's about to burst, our toddler has a full-blown fit and refuses to move out of the candy aisle. People pass by staring daggers. *Can't you*

How to Keep People from Calling Child Services When You're in Public

Maintain a poker face.

Emote gentle concern.

Stand to the side and wring your hands.

Don't give in to your urge to drag your screaming and/or limp child through the mall.

Give in and buy the damn kid the lollipop.

control your brat? they seem to say. *What kind of parent are you, anyway?* Admit it, when you see a particularly ugly tantrum thrown by somebody else's kid, even your teeth are set on edge, and even though you know better, you pass judgment. *Zoons! What a monster that kid is!*

Unfortunately, you'll have to learn how to deal with this kind of embarrassment. The tendency toward total meltdown reaches its zenith at around two and a half years old, and it's possible to go for weeks when every day is one tantrum after the next. Parents without toddlers will be appalled, but you must learn to ignore them if you're ever to let your kid out of her room. As my neighbor Jane told me once, "I learned real quick that I couldn't give a damn what other people think."

What's Up with Tantrums?

Tantrums and toddlers. Kinda synonymous, ain't they? Well, yes, but there's solid reasoning behind it. "It's all about autonomy, seeking independence," says Linda, mom of five-year-old Chandler and three-year-old Mason. "It doesn't matter what the outside situation is. It can be getting into the car seat, or getting dressed in the morning, or not being ready to go out the door. The outside reason is always different, but the inside reasons are the same, and that is, they want to be the one to call the shots."

Not being able to express frustration in words is another culprit, parents in the courtyard think. "I'm always telling him to use his words instead of just screaming," says Laura, mom of two-and-a-half-year-old Cliff. "His tantrums aren't so violent now that he can tell me what he's upset about."

Several parents noted that it wasn't until they had a few more children that they realized a lot of tantrums are kicked off simply by hunger or exhaustion. An overtired toddler is a ticking time bomb waiting to go off, and the most minor infraction will explode him.

We all agree it's hard to be a toddler. "Maybe tantrums are nature's way of reminding us that our babies are becoming their own person," says Misti, mom of two-and-a-half-year-old Amir.

When a toddler is going to tantrum, there's precious little a parent can do about it, we agreed. But there are a few tricks of the trade you can try that might possibly stave off a tantrum.

First, never go anywhere without a fruit bar or other little snack in your bag. When your tot's about to blow, hand him something to eat or drink, and you may be able to get home before the blast occurs.

Second, give him choices to let the toddler feel like he's got some control. "Don't make the choices ultimatums," says Linda, "but real choices. Like, 'You can wear the green shirt or the blue shirt.'" But as any parent of a toddler knows, toddlers sometimes refuse to make a choice. What then? This is where picking your battles comes in. You have to have a very clear sense of what you'll budge on and what you'll not.

"Chandler wore two different shoes to school for a while, because it didn't really matter, and we didn't want to fight her on it," says Linda. "But the car seat wasn't an option. There were times when we'd have to push her down and buckle her in, and we'd drive her to preschool screaming at the top of her lungs."

Yes, it's an exhausting part of raising a toddler, but it's perfectly normal behavior on the child's part, too. "I was really relieved to learn from other parents that my kid wasn't a psycho; she was just a normal toddler," says Kristen, mom of three-year-old Erica. You'd think such knowledge would make us feel better about wrangling a rampaging toddler, wouldn't you?

And Baby Makes Two

I don't care what you say. At some point, you'll volunteer to become the parent of not just one child, but of two or more. That's what the stats say, anyway. According to *American Demographics*, more than 80 percent of American families have more than one child. So this means you're likely to fall prey to the same primal impulses. Join the club.

Allow me to state the obvious by pointing out that adding another child to your household turns you into a completely different parental animal than you were before. Unfortunately, the emphasis here is on the word *animal.*

There's nothing rational about adding another baby to the household when your first child is in the grip of toddlerhood. And yet that is precisely what millions of parents around the world do. Maybe it's the idea of getting it all over with and out of the way in one fell swoop that explains it. The notion that if you can survive five years of hell, everything will be easy to handle until they're all out of the house for college. Or maybe people really think that the only way siblings will play together is if they're spaced exactly two years apart.

Me? I blame hormones.

If you're inclined to have second and third children, then you're highly susceptible to the call of the hormone. Face it, Nature wants us all to be fruitful and multiply, but nobody has told Her that the world is already well populated. So when your baby stops being so completely dependent on you, the hormones creep up and start whispering sweet nothings into your ear. Your first child is almost walking, and suddenly you're thinking that baby blanket's still got a lot of life left in it, and you're simply longing to be pregnant again. You never stop to think about some of the less fun details of pregnancy, like when the smell of coffee makes you vomit, or when you're so huge you can't even haul yourself out of bed to pee anymore without a push from your spouse. You're not thinking of childbirth, either, bag of laughs that that is. Nor can you recall any details of what the first six weeks with a newborn is like. You're certainly not thinking about what stage your firstborn is going to be at when you bring your new bundle home. And this last oversight is your greatest tactical error.

All of the above-mentioned maladies are temporary and can be lived through. But by bringing forth your new baby when your first is a toddler means you've put yourself into a war zone that won't see a cease-fire for several years. And the first year doesn't even count, because they can't fight over the same toy yet.

Here's where parenting really starts to age you. And yet every day millions of otherwise clever families are adding another child to their household when their first is at his or her most volatile.

My friend Nicole just had her third baby. Her two-year-old son, Patrick, formerly a mild-mannered little guy, has gone ballistic, and he now uses screaming as his primary mode of communication. She and her husband don't even speak to each other anymore. They just cope. Barely.

My neighbor Linda had her second child when her first was eighteen months old. Sure, now, at ages five and four, they keep each other company and fall in line with the family routine with a minimum of griping. But what was life like back when the second was first born?

"I don't remember," she says, with a haunted look. Her husband Stafford remembers this much: "Getting ready to go anywhere with both of them was like preparing to summit Everest."

How your toddler will react to a new sibling depends a great deal on what stage your toddler is at.

- **Fifteen months.** This kid is still basically a baby and needs you for nearly everything. She is not going to take kindly to being second-best all of a sudden. Remember, she is on the brink of full-blown toddlerhood, if she's not there already, and she's prepared to do whatever it takes to get your attention back on her, where it belongs. She will climb into your lap and roughly push the newborn away from your breast like just another boring toy. She will find new ways to trash your house. She will stop sleeping through the night, stop eating, and lose whatever interest in potty training she may have had. You're in for some pretty tiring months, I'm afraid. But what the heck were you thinking by getting pregnant again so soon, anyway? You have no one to blame but yourself.

- **Two years.** He's mobile, he's temperamental, and he's got rudimentary powers of reasoning. Hence, you must never let him be alone in a room with the new baby or risk becoming fodder for the kind of crime story people shake their heads at. A displaced two-year-old will merely adjust his attitude to compensate for the loss of attention. Don't you realize that *he* is the king of the universe, not that squalling little red thing in the bassinet? To his mind, this means he must turn up the volume and up the havoc ante so that you have no recourse but to pay attention to him. After all, much like press, good attention or bad attention is still attention. And therefore, it is a goal worth working toward.

- **Three years.** You think you're out of the woods, but you're wrong. Oh, so wrong. A three-year-old faced with her first sibling will take two giant steps backward and revert to an unreasonable two-and-a-half-year-old again. It's not that she's got so much against the baby, which you might succeed in making her think is a giant new toy for her benefit. It's the loss of attention that really ticks her off. Don't try to reuse any of her old baby stuff for this new baby, because she absolutely will not be sharing. No matter if she hasn't looked at that baby blanket in two years, it's *hers*! She'll insist on opening every gift for the new baby and appropriating the items that most interest her, including the blocks and the teethers.

Your entire routine is shattered the moment you bring home your newborn. Your older child will suddenly revert back whole years and refuse to go to sleep, take a bath, get dressed, or eat dinner. He or she is likely to start falling to pieces over the littlest things. Adults in the know will rightly try to pay extra attention to the toddler. They'll come to see the new baby, but bring a big gift for her. The toddler will accept the gift, of course, but she's still painfully aware that she's the displaced one. Even normally easygoing toddlers, and toddlers whom you might think were too old to care about a new baby, act out in alarming ways.

A few weeks after I had my son, I was trying to spend special time with Annie. We had houseguests that week, so Jack was upstairs peacefully sleeping in my girlfriend's competent lap. I asked Annie what she wanted to do and was told, "Let's drive in the car to the Happy Meal place."

Feeling slightly guilty, I agreed too quickly. Fine, I thought. This will be a nice little mother-daughter outing. Several of my friends with two or more children told me that when Jack came, it wouldn't be enough for Luke or others to pay extra attention to Annie; she would need my special attention, too.

A sound theory, but one not easily put into practice. She wasn't a very happy camper, despite the mountain of presents friends and relatives were building for her. And my lack of sleep made me snippy and impatient. She wouldn't go to bed, she wouldn't get out of bed, she wouldn't eat her dinner, she wouldn't eat breakfast, or get dressed, or wear shoes—and all she demanded was candy, candy, candy until I would simply lose it and start yelling. Then we'd have a big tear-fest until I calmed down or Daddy rode to the rescue. We kept excusing her behavior because, after all, there was a new baby in the house. Still, it didn't make our lives any easier.

So I took her to get a Happy Meal, of which I knew she'd eat two Chicken McNuggets and a whole bag of fries and drink half her Coke. Hardly a nutritious lunch, I know. But who among us doesn't hope to placate our upset children with special treats once in a while?

Even though she looked very tired, the trip went well, and afterward I thought I'd make a quick run to the stationery store to find some baby announcements. You'd think I'd have learned by now that you can't push your luck with a tired, hungry child. But I was so flush with a feeling of relative freedom I had to try. Jack was safe with my friend, and I really, really needed to get some birth announcements into the mail for the clamoring relatives. The trouble started when we got to the stationery store and Annie saw a book of stickers she wanted. "Buy this for me, Mommy!" she said, and I shook my head. We have lots of stickers at home, I told her, and we don't have money for this right now. And besides, we don't have to buy something every time we come into a store.

My logic was lost on her. She refused to put them back. I tried reasoning with her, which any parent of a toddler knows is futile, but which we all try anyway, hoping to be progressive and give our kid the benefit of the doubt. Next, I tried my stern Mommy tone: "Annie, put down the book right now, please." No go. Then I tried my "I'll count to three" voice, which usually works, but didn't this time, so I was left to try to grab the sticker book from her hands, and before long we were in a full-blown power struggle. I hate public tantrums. I feel like everyone is watching (which they are) and judging my parental abilities (which they probably are) as I try to contain the situation. After a tearful ten minutes, I managed to get her out of the store and onto an outside bench, where I got another Chicken McNugget into her. We were almost back at the car when she pitched into tantrum number two. Something about a ladybug? She wanted to see the ladybug? She threw herself down onto the parking lot pavement, screaming that she didn't want to go home, and I finally had to hoist all forty kicking, howling pounds of her into the car seat by myself so that traffic could finally move past. Did I mention that I'd just had a baby three weeks earlier?

Home was only a five-minute drive away, but it seemed like an hour. My shirt front was soaking with leaking milk, and I had a pounding headache. When was the last time I'd eaten? Who the heck had time to eat with two kids? Jack was just starting to cry for a feeding when I walked in the door, but Annie was still in the car, having refused to get out of her car seat. Fortunately, my friend handed over the baby and went downstairs to deal with Annie.

Oh, what had I done? What had I done, I moaned, as I tried to nurse a screaming baby. Annie arrived upstairs and immediately threw herself on the ground before me. My friend offered to make us all lunch, and I proceeded to beg her to stay with me forever. I'll pay you rent if you could just stay on my futon in the living room for the next six months, I told her. She was sympathetic, but wisely declined. Can you blame her?

Sharing and Other Myths

Let's just get the official stuff over with. According to all the experts, most children are not developmentally ready to engage in parallel play until they're at least three years old. That means that for most of the toddler population, sharing is a concept whose time has not yet come.

And yet sharing (or not) is one of the concepts that comes to mind quickest when discussing toddlers and their foibles. On the measuring stick of civilization, sharing ranks right up there with potty training. Parents start invoking its name as soon as they introduce their children to other children.

But look at it from a toddler's point of view. They've only just learned the joys of ownership, and now we want them to give up their prized possessions. Nor are they clear on what objects we ask them to share that they can expect to get back. We ask Sammy to please share the dolls with Carla, but also to share the cookies as well. Unless Carla's not eating that particular kind of cookie this week, that "shared" cookie won't be coming back to its original owner. This much Sammy understands. So why share the dolls?

And yet *sharing* is the verb most often heard on playgrounds and in day-care yards across the country (along with the admonishment to STOP BITING!). Experienced parents know that sharing is more an ideal to work toward rather than an ironclad rule to observe at every play gathering, so they don't get too upset when the invariable happens: toddler lock.

Toddler lock is when two or more toddlers converge on the same toy and refuse to let go. It's never a pleasant sight, and depending on the personalities of the toddlers involved, it will turn into a hitting or biting match before adults can break it up. No matter who's involved, it always ends in tears.

Unfortunately, there's not a lot you as a parent can do for toddler lock besides remove the offending toy. Even if Bobby was playing with the truck first when Jake came and laid claim to it, Jake, in his current incarnation as a toddler, will never understand why that's a problem. If you take it away from Jake, Jake will start to scream and cry. If you take it away from Bobby, he will start to scream and cry.

Your only option is to remove the toy, as mentioned earlier, and try to divert both toddlers' attention to something else. Of course, now they're both screaming and crying. But if you can divert them—and by this juncture you know all about the tactical wisdom of diversion, right?—they'll soon forget about the truck.

But that's Bobby's favorite truck, you say? In that case, it's best not to bring it out at all. The same goes for your toddler's favorite "thing," his special comfort doll or blanket. There are lots of more neutral toys to practice sharing with. Why make life more difficult?

In the meantime, continue talking up the values of sharing to your toddler, even if she can't quite put it into practice yet. At some point she will be able to share her toys with others, not always graciously, maybe, but grudgingly, at least. And by the time she's in elementary school, she'll have the notion, if not the action, down pat.

Tradition!

We Americans do so love a good tradition. And we have so many to choose from. The problem comes when it's time to decide whose tradition to cleave to, his or hers or theirs or some others that you just randomly made up a few years ago.

There are no doubt many parents who fire up the household tradition database the day after their first child is born. This, in my estimation, is silly, since the baby won't take any notice of your Aunt Sarah's amazing *matzo brei* or your *Elvis Sings Father Christmas* LPs. It's my humble opinion that in matters of family tradition left ignored until now, it's best to wait until the kid can at least notice what's going on. In general, this means the toddler years.

My rule of thumb is this: everything can wait until the third year. Think of it as a two-year preparation course.

Of course, this presents unique problems of its own. Your average toddler isn't the most gracious participant in events that celebrate peace and family harmony. The concept of giving rather than receiving is utterly lost on him. In general, toddlers don't do well at functions that require sitting still, asking questions on cue, and keeping their fingers out of the olives. They don't like wearing scratchy new outfits you buy for the occasion. They don't like being pinched by really old people they don't remember ever seeing before. Most of all, they don't like being told that all those colorful presents under the tree are not for them.

Still, they are now officially at an age when they can respond to your attempts to introduce them to family tradition, even if that response is not what you had in mind. So starting in the toddler years, you begin to fret about what, if any, traditions to indoctrinate junior with. After all, when we think back on our own childhoods, lots of us can dimly remember holiday-related traumas of late toddlerhood, so the same must be true of our own progeny.

And so we jump. Traditions we've forgotten or purposely ignored since we moved away from home we now take out and dust off like so many Christmas tree ornaments. It doesn't matter what background or religion you admit to. The symptoms are all the same. If you remember Frank Sinatra singing "I Saw Mommy Kissing Santa Claus," you'll dutifully go out and search the used-record stores for your own copy. (Or more likely, since you've got a toddler underfoot, you'll cop for the easiest route and buy one online. The guys who invented the World Wide Web probably had no idea how valuable online shopping would be to parents.) Your husband will start pining for just the kind of mince pie his mom used to make, and he'll proceed to make your life hell until you can either learn how to make it yourself or find the one shop in town that makes it (and it will never be as good). You may attempt to cook a turkey for the first time in your life. Problems will plague you in these attempts. Last holiday I got the silly notion into my head that I would roast some chestnuts. Nobody told me that I had to puncture the shells in some way before putting them into the oven, and I spent the next week cleaning chestnut shrapnel out of my oven.

Some traditions are more knowledge-intensive than others. I have many Jewish friends who knew less about Judaism than your average Baptist preacher until they had children. Then it was a mad scramble to get back up to speed. They enrolled in classes. Their spouses converted. They'd dust off the Hanukkah songbook for the first time in years and ponder the question, "Just where does one get a shank bone in this town, anyway?" In a traditional Jewish seder, or Passover dinner, the youngest child is called upon to ask Four Questions, including the all-important, "Why is this night unlike any other night?" (Hint: it has to do with the Jews being led out of slavery in Egypt.) As soon as their child is talking at all, they spend countless hours getting him to utter those four phrases—which the child will happily do until the guests arrive and the seder is in progress. Then he'll clamp shut.

The interfaith couple has particular problems when it comes to deciding which holiday traditions to celebrate. My friends Tori and Jon are a good example. Tori comes from Minnesota, where her family celebrated Christmas in the kind of way only viewed on TV Christmas specials or in a Martha Stewart book. Lots of elegant handmade home decorations, a giant tree bent over under the weight of hundreds of heirloom ornaments, roasting ham in the oven, and apple pies cooling on the countertop. Jon, on the other hand, comes from an Orthodox Jewish tradition, and although he's still deeply ambivalent about how Jewish he really wants to be, he can't abide any Christmas decorations of any kind in his home. So he's dusted off the menorah and the Hanukkah songbook so he can make an impression on his daughter, who might wonder why her parents glower at each other all December while she's enjoying both the apple pies *and* the potato latkes.

Sometimes, neither of you have any particular traditions, but you want to have something for your toddler to remember his Decembers by, so you must invent some. I have some friends who celebrate all the solstices with elaborate meals based on the produce of the season. They read some poems. They recite some of the history behind the seasonal changes. Last time I spoke with them, however, their three-year-old wanted to know why Santa Claus didn't come to their house.

I Saw Mommy Slipping Santa Claus a $5

The problem with a lot of traditions in this country is that the big brand-name holidays now have very little to do with religion and everything to do with shopping. You can try to insulate your two-year-old as long as you can, but believe me, once the kid gets out into the world of day care or preschool, the holidays come to them.

The marketers are no dummies. They know that everything about Christmas is geared toward children: the bright lights, the candies, the big fat man who brings them presents. They also know that no parent can resist dusting off the Christmas cheer when confronted by an awestruck child, especially their own, experiencing it for the first time.

Last year I went to a sort of holiday family reunion with far-flung cousins. We brought all the kids together for the first time at Christmas. They were all under five, and it was a real sight to see the new generation running around and wearing olives on their fingers, just as we had twenty-five years earlier. Everything was smashing, except I couldn't keep my eyes off the growing pile of presents under the giant tree—a tree so big it never would have fit in my apartment, much less in the front door of the building. When we put the kids to bed that night, I could see the trouble we were headed into. The pile under the tree continued to grow until it was a veritable mountain of green and red wrapping paper and silver bows. There were bags of smaller toys and candy that we stuffed into their stockings. Then there were the "oversized" items that fit neither under the tree nor into a stocking, but were covered by a sheet in the hallway instead. None of our kids, all middle-class, all with rooms already stuffed with clothes and toys and books, really needed anything that was under that tree, but we couldn't stop ourselves. We had to give them the whole experience, from the chocolate Santa Claus figures to the packs of new underwear.

In the morning, my worst fears were confirmed. We gave them their stockings first, and if we'd had any decency and sense of restraint, we would have stopped there and the kids would never have known the difference. In their giant stockings was stuffed everything a kid under five wanted—candies, toy cars, little people, little animals, little books, dinosaurs. And they played happily for about half an hour before some of us adults got impatient and announced that there was *more*. That's when things got ugly.

The kids ripped into their presents as fast as we could hand them over. Each gift got a brief glance before being tossed aside with one hand while the other reached out for the next. "What's next?" became the call of the day. As you'd expect, when we came to the end of the pile (it was a long time coming), all kids simultaneously broke down into frenzied sobs. "We want more presents!" they sobbed like little orphans. "More!"

Five Reasons to Avoid the Holidays When You Have a Toddler

1. Ignoring the holidays means you won't have to travel with a toddler, a unique brand of hell in and of itself.
2. You think a toddler is going to eat turkey, stuffing, and cranberry sauce?
3. At Christmas, toddlers are very quick to prefer quantity over quality.
4. You won't have to be subjected to the Barney Thanksgiving special or other misguided specials on TV.
5. You won't feel compelled to spend a lot of money.

I was left wondering what the whole point of that particular holiday was. The part about meeting cousins and running screaming through the house with each other was great. Even the stuffing themselves senseless with goodies I could live with, as long as it was tempered with a more nutritious breaking of bread around the table with relatives. But I didn't approve of the big, neon MORE blinking overhead. Its only purpose, as far as I could see, was to create good little consumers as early as possible.

This year I'm taking my daughter to the main post office downtown, where they keep all the letters to Santa Claus written by little kids and sent via charity. We'll pick out one or two from kids whose only want is for a ball, or a singular Power Ranger, or a doll with long hair, and give those kids a Christmas. I'm hoping I can instill in my daughter a sense that giving is indeed better than receiving. I just hope I'm not too late.

When introducing toddlers to beloved traditions, it's best not to have any expectations of how they'll react. This way, you'll be less ticked off when they react badly.

Scream III

I went to the ends of the earth to get Annie her Halloween costume. OK, I exaggerate. But I did drive into the hills. Until now, Annie and Halloween had the most tenuous of relationships. At almost one, when she was still pliant and yielding to my dress code, I put her in a little clown outfit and wheeled her around town to the adoring coos of passersby. At almost two, I got her a very cute Winnie the Pooh suit that I thought might double as a sleeper. She ignored it, and on Halloween night, fought me tooth and claw until I finally gave up. We have one picture of her in this outfit. It shows Luke forcibly holding up the hood with bear ears and Annie trying to pull it back off, grimacing. We didn't go trick-or-treating that year.

I have great memories of Halloween. It was the biggest holiday of the year in my book. My neighborhood was stuffed with kids, and we spent weeks planning our costumes (and the secondary costumes, so we could go back out for a second round). The thought of introducing my own progeny to this great American tradition excited me.

By the time she was nearly three, I figured she was ready for some serious Halloween action. I thought up several complicated outfits, and even briefly entertained the idea of sewing a cape and apron for a Little Red Riding Hood ensemble myself. Never mind that the last thing I'd sewn was a pillow for my junior high home economics class. Never mind that I don't own a sewing machine, much less pinking shears, much less the floor space necessary to even cut out a pattern. And never mind that since I was working full-time at that point, I didn't have time to cook dinner, much less sew a costume. After thinking about the costume for two months, I did what most working mothers do: I opted to buy a bee costume instead. A mom advertised her daughter's old costume on a local parents' E-mail newsletter I subscribe to, and I bit.

I drove into the wealthy Kensington area, in the hills above Berkeley, where the houses are far off the lots and the house numbers are covered by lush, imported foliage. I finally found the house, wandered up, and knocked. A smiling little girl appeared at the leaded glass door, closely followed by a scowling, older woman, who raised her eyebrows at me, indicating that I should identify myself before she would consider opening the door. Fair enough. These are scary times, and although I don't consider myself particularly scary-looking, maybe I was having a bad hair day. And keep in mind, I was there to inquire about a little bee costume.

"I've come about the bee costume?"

She let me in. After the briefest of exchanges, the bee costume was mine, and a $15 check was hers. The door slammed shut behind me.

I got the bee costume home, and set about making an elaborate set of bee wings out of coat hangers and gauze and glue. I figured I could just sew it somehow onto the back of the costume or attach it with some Velcro.

Annie wouldn't wear it. If she battled the Pooh costume at two, she'd perfected the art of war by three. First, I had to catch her. Then I had to pin her down and stuff her into a tight bee costume and get her headband on. As soon as I had one arm in, she had the other arm out. The headband was ripped from her head mere seconds after I'd attached it. She kicked, she bit, she screamed. Once again, I wondered how people go about actually kidnapping toddlers, since one risks serious bodily harm making them do something they really don't want to do. We went on in this tit-for-tat matter for several minutes, until finally I realized that I was losing this battle. Then it was my turn to pout. "Fine!" I yelled as she twisted out of her costume for the last time. "Don't wear a costume for Halloween! All the other kids will be in a costume except for you and I DON'T CARE!"

But parenthood is about second chances. And third chances. And chances into perpetuity. So after I calmed down a little, and seeing that she was actually wearing her little black tights, I tried another tact, reasoning that she really did want to dress up for Halloween this year—she just didn't realize it yet.

I pulled out a little black skirted leotard she'd shown favor to in recent weeks and tried to interest her in putting it on. She agreed. Great, I thought. Now she can be a Playboy Bunny, or a cat, or a whatever. At least she looks like she's dressed up. I sacrificed a pair of my own black tights, chopping one of the legs off to fashion a kitty tail, and then searched the apartment for a safety pin. Then I tried to draw whiskers on her face. Wrong move. Never invade a testy three-year-old's space.

"No! Go away! No!" I got two whiskers on her right side drawn before she escaped me. As I stood in front of the mirror with my broken $20 Clinique eyeliner, calming myself down, Annie went out to look at the kids downstairs in their costumes. Then she peed in her pants and came back to show me how her shoes had filled up to the top.

So Annie went trick-or-treating in leggings and a sweater, never noticing that she was the only kid not dressed up. I went with her, growling to myself how I would never do this again. I'm nobody's patsy, I muttered to myself. I'm not going out of my way for anything like this ever again. A few weeks later, my day-care lady presented me with a photo she'd taken the day of Halloween, and there was Annie, beaming in her bee costume. Indeed, Annie talked about being a bee for months afterward, even though she wasn't a bee for Halloween.

This next year she'll be almost four, and she's showing a lot more promise. She says she wants to be a fairy ballerina, and my neighbor has already set me up with a tutu and wings her toddler son has lost interest in. Annie has also already adorned our front door with many variations on ghost and spider themes. Meanwhile, my son is a perfectly pliant three-month-old, who'll have no opinion whatsoever on my dressing him up as an amoeba or dust mite. Halloween may work out this year after all, and I'll have no one to blame but myself for the ten pounds of candy she's sure to bring home.

Birthday Parties

I was never a believer in the big first birthday party. I always felt that if you're going to drop a wad of cash on a party for a baby who doesn't know the difference between a cake and a watermelon, you clearly have too much money on your hands. Better to admit the party is for yourself, in celebration of getting through the inaugural year of parenthood, and have your own friends over for pizza and beer. No one-year-old is going to ask about a cake, much less presents. Does she really need more toys, anyway?

Nobody else thinks like this, however. I recently declined one friend's invitation to go to her one-year-old's party at Chuck E. Cheese's because I knew what kind of afternoon it would degenerate into: there would be mediocre pizza, a mountain of presents (leading to a tedious hour or so trying to get the one-year-old to unwrap them all by himself), and, at the end of the day, a bunch of hysterical babies crying because the mechanical mice sang them "Happy Birthday."

I told her I had a root canal that day. Sorry.

Another friend had a much better solution. She merely had a picnic in the park with her friends, with a token cake to mark the occasion. In lieu of presents, all the adults merely brought their blessings to her daughter. There wasn't a screaming baby in sight.

A two-year-old can still be lulled into thinking his birthday is a day like any other, but the pressures on you as parents pull harder. Now you've got a walking, screaming, semi-person, everyone notes. Don't you want to celebrate the tremendous milestone of the second year? Wouldn't he enjoy a party? He's a little boy, after all.

The temptation is there to throw a really big party. With clowns and horses and balloons. But in reality, nothing will freak your two-year-old out more. In fact, the amount of money you spend on entertainment is guaranteed to be directly proportional to the level of hysteria the tot works himself into. It will be an exhausting day for everyone involved, and there's no indication your two-year-old will remember any of it. Why bother?

Even if you're a misanthrope and manage to withstand the social pressure to throw your small child a major bash, you'll probably have to succumb for the all-important third birthday. A three-year-old is just socialized enough to not only know what a birthday party is, but also to expect one. He'll have been listening to his day-care friends describe the dog-and-pony shows their parents have thrown for them in years past, plus he'll be watching various skits involving birthday parties on TV at day care. You know you're done for when he comes home and asks you when his birthday is, and then upon learning this information, tells you what he expects to receive when it comes. If you think this is bad, just wait. Four-year-olds spend most of their year planning their fifth birthday party. One of the girls in our courtyard invites and disinvites people to her party all year long, depending on who's in her favor at the moment.

It's true that sooner or later you'll have to throw a birthday party, but it still doesn't mean you have to hire clowns and ponies and rent jumping bags.

Toddler Birthday Fun

Help me in my nationwide campaign to put an end to ridiculously lavish toddler birthday parties. Restore common sense! Here are some cheap and easy ideas for spending your toddler's big birthday bash:

- **Have cupcakes instead of cake.** They're easy to make, easy to decorate, and from a toddler's point of view, a little personal cake all his or her own.

- **Pizza.** A couple of cheese pizzas and otherwise forbidden soda pop will thrill most two- and three-year-olds to the gills.

- **A guitar.** There isn't a toddler on earth who doesn't love song and dance. Find someone who can pick out a couple of kids' tunes and get the whole group singing along.

- **Beach party.** Make sandwiches, bring juice boxes, and have everyone meet at the beach for some fun in the sun. Hand out bucket/shovel sets purchased at a drugstore for 99 cents as your party favor, and watch the kids go to town. Don't forget the sunscreen!

In the lore of toddler birthday parties, the common wisdom is this: one guest for each year of life. That is, if your kid is two, invite two friends, and so on. It's a very sensible rule, and if anyone paid it any attention, they might actually experience a toddler birthday party that did not include a mass meltdown and lots of screaming.

Unfortunately, you usually can't abide by this golden rule, even if you want to. The reason? Invitation guilt.

Invitation Guilt

There is a big problem with getting your toddler out into the real world to mingle with others of his ilk. This problem is invitation guilt.

Here's how it happens. Your child becomes very good friends with everyone in his play group or day care. One of his little friends invites him to his birthday party, and you buy a gift and take him to the big day. When your child's next birthday comes around, you naturally have to invite that child and his parent, because they invited you. Within a year, you can expect to suddenly find yourself on the receiving end of hundreds of reciprocal invitations to birthday parties, clogging up your every weekend for the next year and forcing you to enter a giant toy superstore and spend money on presents you have no idea if the kid wants or not.

This vicious circle extends to you as well, naturally. When your toddler's big birthday comes around, he naturally wants to invite everyone. You queasily count up the number of children plus one parent and wonder how much you'll have to fork over to Chuck E. Cheese's. Then come the RSVPs, and lo and behold, the other parent also plans to attend. (Everyone loves a birthday party.) Although the number of party favor bags stays constant, it means twice as much pizza, cake, ice cream, and beverages—and the need for twice as much space. Now your whole party budget is blown, and you're forced to contemplate two options: cough up the cash or start uninviting people. Or you can do neither and hope flu season comes early and knocks a few people out.

Invitation guilt is probably the main culprit behind why toddler birthday parties get so out of control. You may really want to show restraint and keep it down to one or two kids and their parents, but you simply have to invite every kid at day care or risk becoming a social pariah, unable to look the other parents in the eye.

Get used to it. It's just another hazard of parenting a toddler, an unfortunate by-product of civilization.

So now your little ball of terror is starting to take on a few basic character traits of a human being. You deserve some credit for helping him along. But don't get too cocky just yet. Just because he's starting to age out of the toddler era doesn't mean your job is done. Far from it, my friends. Keep reading.

I SPIT ON YOUR TRICYCLE

Parenting the Older Toddler

*"Ask your child what he wants for dinner
only if he's buying."*
—**Fran Lebowitz**

Parents everywhere heave a huge sigh of relief on the day of their child's third birthday. The Terrible Twos are over, they hurrah. Now their child is no longer an unpredictable toddler. Her personality will revert back to its former sweetness and light, and she'll be generally agreeable and help them with the housework.

Tragically, your hopes are often dashed at the very birthday party you've thrown to celebrate this bright new era. You

171

can hire a clown, invite the day-care friends, decorate the house with "Blue's Clues" paraphernalia, and buy a very big and elaborate cake, only to watch helplessly as the whole production degenerates into a screaming, crying, petulant mess.

Three-year-olds are still toddlers. They're just bigger, smarter, and more agile. In short, they're at the top of their game. You're not back in Kansas yet, my pretties.

Portrait of a Three-Year-Old

Your average three-year-old is a much more evolved creature than the two-year-old. She's looking less like a baby every day. She may start out this fourth year of life with some of

The Top Ten Myths About Three-Year-Olds

1. Everything will be OK now.
2. Your three-year-old wants to please you.
3. All three-year-olds are potty-trained.
4. Three-year-olds start eating again.
5. Three-year-olds can share.
6. Three-year-olds adapt well to new siblings.
7. A three-year-old can tell you what happened.
8. A three-year-old is ready to wear normal clothes again.
9. A three-year-old can pick up her own room.
10. A three-year-old is much easier than a two-year-old.

that cute baby fat hanging around the belly, but she'll leave it with the sturdy, strong muscles of a bona fide little kid as she approaches four. Indeed, three years is the portal between a toddler and a kid. She can climb stairs like a grownup. She can swing a bat with deadly accuracy. This is the year she'll master a tricycle, or even a bigger bike with training wheels. She can dress and undress herself at will. In fact, chasing down your naked three-year-old will occupy many an hour in the next twelve months. Just as she's physically more developed, her little mind is developing as well, often in alarming ways. She no longer needs to throw a tantrum at the slightest provocation; she waits until it is strategically ideal to throw one, like in front of dinner guests, when she knows you are most likely to give in quickly. She understands you and your weak spots better than your therapist, and she's consummately skilled at pitting the two of you against each other to get what she wants (usually more cookies). She still embraces the toddler's basic credo: "It's all about me," but she supplements it with uncanny cunning. Sound scary? It is.

That said, three-year-olds are also enchanting. They're closely watching and mimicking what they see around them. You can watch them turning into the people they're destined to be: the girl with the beat, the boy who loves books. Three is also the year of imagination overload. It's the year when monsters and talking dogs and pillow witches take up residence in their rooms. It's the year they start asking you to explain everything and to let them see all that you're doing. You'll often be surprised to find yourself holding conversations with your three-year-old, in whole sentences, trying to explain everyday occurrences in simple terms which, unbeknownst to you she already has a grasp on.

She: Let's get some ice cream.

You: We can't right now. We don't have any cash.

She: Well just go to the bank and get some.

You: (aghast) Uh, it doesn't work that way.

She: Why not? That's what Daddy does. Use your card.

And so on. And you'll shake your head and wonder, "Where did my baby suddenly go?" That little boy who couldn't pronounce "spaghetti"? Oh, he's still there, but he mostly comes out when sick, or when he's had a nightmare (three-year-olds have lots of these), or when you're called upon to spray his room for monsters.

The Truth About Three-Year-Olds

It's a curious fact, but you'll notice that none of the parenting books reveal the truth about three-year-olds. Is it a conspiracy? Do they think we won't be able to cope with the truth but will leave our children on church doorsteps instead? Like the myth of acne suddenly clearing up by eighteen (I'm thirty-six and still waiting, thank you), the common wisdom is that your reward for having survived a whole year of two-year-old tantrums is a mature and sweet-natured three-year-old. What you really get is a much smarter, much craftier, and in many respects a much more cranky two-year-old. You get a toddler who you can no longer contain during a tantrum. You get a toddler who can get in and out of his own car seat, and who would have no problem opening the car door when you're on the road, except that your screaming scared him the last time he tried.

Common wisdom also holds that if your toddler didn't really go through a "terrible" second year, you're in for it when she hits three. The thrust for independence that is at the root of so much toddler turmoil hits some toddlers later than others.

Most parents confess to complete shell shock when faced with a rampaging three-year-old. They let their guard down and weren't mentally prepared for the onslaught. You can usually identify these poor souls by their startled looks. They'd been planning on their child phasing out of the toddler phase this year, but with each passing month, that disappointment grows as their three-year-old continues on in much the same vein, and sometimes even worse. *Nobody told us about this,* they whisper to any who will listen. *We weren't prepared.*

Sorry. Nobody said this parenting gig was easy.

That said, at least you're experienced. Imagine if nature unleashed a three-year-old on you as soon as your baby started walking. Few would survive. At least you're facing another year of toddlerhood after two years of training in the field. You understand toddlers better than you think.

You know, for example, that three-year-olds are still ruled by their sleep schedules and their stomachs, so you still have some sort of road map to their moods. A three-year-old might fairly trip to preschool in the morning, excited to see her friends and practice drawing, but when you pick her up, she's reverted back to a two-year-old. She's tired, she's hungry, and she's going to start a fight no matter what you do to placate her. She'll skillfully manipulate her bedtime until it's almost your bedtime as well, even though she's swaying on her feet and she's got purple bags under her eyes.

Affection—or Manipulation?

Three-year-olds are such good manipulators that even we parents can't tell when they're being genuine versus when they want something. They understand how cute we think they are. They know that if they say sweet things, we're more likely to cave in to demands. They have a whole portfolio of phrases they know get a rise out of us, and they employ them in carefully thought-out schemes to get us to come running. Fortunately, crafty though they are, they're still only three years old. Hopefully, you'll catch on quick next time you hear one of these:

- **"Thank you for being such a nice mommy."** Wait for the punch line, folks. There's sure to be one.
- **"Daddy, I'm scared!"** Highly suspect when it's broad daylight, and you're trying to read the paper.
- **"Mommy, I'm hungry!"** But not for the food you served for dinner that I didn't eat.
- **"I just want to see them!"** Said indignantly as she fingers the cookie bag.
- **"Daddy, could I have a hug?"** And then could I have some more of your chips?

Nonrested, a three-year-old is as prone to tantrum throwing as the most volatile two-and-a-half-year-old. Many of the same conundrums set her off—the laws of physics and gravity insult her daily. But after a good night's sleep, or after one of her increasingly rare naps, she may be surprisingly reasonable about things. I remember running out of Cheerios one morning and dreading the tantrum my daughter was sure to throw. But to my shock, she calmly accepted my explanation of the situation and agreed to eat an egg instead. Her future persona flashed before my eyes briefly, and it took me several minutes to recover. It's these rare glimpses you have to cling to to survive this final year of toddlerhood.

The Art of the Deal

Three years old is a time fraught with danger for parents of toddlers. By definition, a three-year-old is hardly a toddler anymore. They've mastered their bodies in alarming ways. They can run, climb up and down stairs, jump backward like bunnies—all the sorts of things that tire you out just thinking about them. They've also grasped the finer points of negotiation and manipulation. They get what they want out of you not through mere screaming, although they'll resort to that when cornered, but through crafty, personalized deal-making.

Everything is negotiable in the eyes of the older toddler. Take bedtime, for example. Three-year-olds know when their bedtime is and have mastered many subtle ways of extending it for another full hour. *At least* a full hour. The "I need a drink of water" and "Read me another book" tricks are for the younger set. A three-year-old will employ arguments that would impress a trial lawyer.

When Do I Get My Toddler a "Big Kid" Bed?

Ah, the big kid bed. A real milestone if ever there was one. You can't help but wipe a tear of nostalgia from your eye as you dismantle the crib you spent so much care choosing two years ago. That said, it can be a pretty exciting time for both you and your toddler—providing your toddler is ready and waiting for his very own big kid bed.

How do you know when your toddler is ready for the big leagues? There is no right age, members of the Toddler Summit agree. In fact, when you shift depends a lot on you.

Stafford and Linda's first child, Chandler, got bumped from her crib at eighteen months when her brother Mason came along. By the time Mason was two, they grew tired of bending over the bar to lay him down, and put him in a bed as well. They solved the obvious big bed problem by using futons on the floor. It's hard to plummet from a futon.

Other parents simply take their cue from the child. Once a toddler can crawl out of his crib, it's just as easy to have a big kid bed. This can be anywhere from eighteen months to three years, depending on the child. Annie never climbed out of her crib, but at around two she stopped sleeping comfortably. There was a lot of thrashing around during the night, whereas before she'd slept soundly. We got her a twin bed rather than a toddler bed because I didn't see the point in switching beds twice.

Picture this scenario. It's 9 P.M. Bedtime for your three-and-a-half-year-old. You've bathed him, read him his two favorite books, tucked him in with his favorite bear. You think you're off the hook, but the bargaining is just beginning.

A good twin bed would last her ten or more years, so why not get her used to it now? Toddler beds are for the feeble who need a halfway point between crib and bed, and, since your toddler will grow out of it in a few short years, they are just another excuse to spend money.

Everyone agrees that you can lead a toddler to bed, but you can't make him sleep. Jane and Luis got their daughter Claudia a big girl bed mostly as a ruse to get her to stop making a bedtime-delaying scene from her crib. It worked wonders for a while, until she decided she wanted to "camp" on her floor in a Winnie the Pooh sleeping bag, like she had at her cousin's house. This lasted for weeks, until Luis got the bright idea to put the sleeping bag on top of her bed and told her she could camp there just as easily. She's been sleeping in it ever since.

It's true that toddlers do sleep in active ways. I've found my daughter on the floor at the end of the bed plenty of times on my midnight bathroom run/kid check. But she seems no worse for the wear. Keep the mattress close to the floor if you want to minimize the fall factor. Or install safety rails until she's old enough not to need them anymore.

How do you know a toddler has accepted his bed? He'll incorporate it into his play. It will become the savanna for his menagerie, a stage for his dolls, a place to pile his books, or, the universal sign of bed love: it will become his personal trampoline.

"Daddy," he'll say very sweetly, "will you leave the hall light on?"

"Sure," you say. Why not? "But go to sleep now."

"But I want to finish reading my book."

"No, mister, you need to go to sleep now. You can look at your books again tomorrow."

"But Daddy, what do you and Mommy do when I go to sleep?"

"We watch TV or we read." You clear your throat. "But we're the grownups."

"But I like to read so much."

"I know, honey. But it's time to go to sleep."

"Can I stay in bed and look at one more book?"

You pause, thinking what's the harm if he stays in bed, right?

Your three-year-old knows he has you now. That one book will turn into four or five. Then he'll slip out of bed and be playing in the closet next time you check in on him at 11 P.M. Then he'll tell you that he's in the middle of this really good chapter, and can't he have just five more minutes? It's child's play for him. Worst of all, he's learning this stuff from you!

Food is another favorite subject for negotiation. Older toddlers know very well what you'll let them get away with and what you won't, so they'll try a variety of clever ruses to trip you up.

"I want some more marshmallows, Mommy."

"No. One bowl is plenty."

"Please? They taste so good."

I dunno. This one worked on me. That they tasted good was so . . . true and rational that I caved in and gave her another (small) bowl of marshmallows. Call me weak. My kid just knows me too well.

A good round of negotiations, successful or not, makes a normal three-year-old giddy with power. Imagine: going mano a mano with Mommy or Daddy and actually getting them to consider your proposal. It's heady stuff! And so, three-year-olds, being the self-obsessed creatures they are, will try to negotiate the terms for everything in their lives. This includes routines they don't much care for, such as bedtime and bathtime, as well as privileges they enjoy, such as video watching or having a snack. They will always try to get a little something extra out of you, and this makes them seem, well, alarmingly selfish. And they are, until you remember that they're just doing their job by testing to see how far they can push you.

> *You:* All right. Here's a cherry Popsicle for you.
>
> *Him:* When I eat this, can I have an orange Popsicle next?
>
> *You:* No.
>
> *Him:* Please?
>
> *You:* No.
>
> *Him:* Then can I eat my cherry Popsicle and watch a video?
>
> *You:* Don't push it, buster.
>
> *Him:* (having eaten half the cherry Popsicle, he places it on the table in front of you) I don't like cherry. I want an orange one.

You let them go outside for ten minutes, and they'll ignore your calls for twenty minutes after that. (My daughter parrots back at me: "Just a minute, Mommy, I'm working."

Yikes! Wonder where she got that? *Ahem.*) You let them watch one video, but still they agitate for another one just before bedtime. You offer to read her one book at bedtime, and she always asks for two more. You're constantly negotiating the rules with your three-year-old. It's a lot like living with a used-car salesman with a really bad temper.

It's important to keep to your guns, however. Remember consistency and discipline? They come into play here in a big way. Once you've set a rule, you can't bend, even once, or your three-year-old will never *ever* let you forget that once you did let her eat her dinner in front of the TV, so why not now? Your waffling in a weak moment will only serve to make your toddler more persistent, more relentless, in her deal-making with you. So draw your line in the sand, and don't let your toddler cross it. Or else.

Whine List

Older toddlers have mostly overcome the communication barrier. They can make their desires known without scream-ing. They can pronounce most words in a way that is more or less understandable. They understand what you are saying to them most of the time (whether they choose to listen is another subject). But older toddlers develop a secondary way to communicate with those around them. It's the middle way between talking and crying. And pound for pound, it's more effective than either.

They whine.

Whining is a dangerous game from a Darwinian standpoint. An afternoon of whining will drive even the most patient parent to rage. And yet, all three-year-olds whine. The experts tell us that toddlers whine when they're bored or they feel they need attention. (I must have one heck of a bored toddler.) I posit that whining is merely the most effective way to get a reaction out of a grownup, and as such, toddlers do it. Incessantly.

Combine whining with repetition, and you have a recipe for success, toddler-style.

"Maw-MEEEEEE. I want this book." It's a whiny sing-song that strikes dread into the heart of an experienced toddler parent.

Allow me to translate. What it means is this: "I want this book now, and even though you're going to say that I have too many books like this one at home already, I'm not going to take no for an answer. I'm prepared to throw a public Force Three tantrum and force you to drag me out of here to the car, which I understand is parked some ways away, forcing you to forgo your own enjoyable book browsing and ultimate book purchase. In short, if you do not buy me this book, I am prepared to ruin your evening."

What do you do? Buying her another Berenstain Bears book is a small price to pay for half an hour of peace and quiet. You know it, and she knows that you know it.

Fortunately, there are one or two techniques you can try to emasculate a growing whine.

"I can't hear you when you're whining." My neighbor Misti employs this to excellent results whenever her toddler son starts to whine. Amir will whine for another few minutes, realize his mother isn't listening, then switch into a mode proven to work. "Mommy, can I please have . . ." and voilà, Mommy pays attention.

Whine back. By three years, toddlers are starting to show their sense of humor. It's possible to diffuse a rapidly deteriorating situation by mimicking your three-year-old's whine and lightening the mood.

"Mommeeee, I wanna go now. . . ."

"Annieeee, I just gotta pay for thiiiis, then we can goooooo."

She laughs. I laugh. People in line give us the fish eye, and everyone gets to avoid a tantrum.

Beware, however. Some three-year-olds still take themselves very seriously and do not appreciate being mocked. If you've got this kind of toddler, attempt this technique at your peril.

Meanwhile, get used to whining. Tragically, whining works so well in so many situations that many toddlers never grow out of it. You probably know a few peers who get what they want via whining. Funny thing, it's just as irritating in an adult.

Misguided Adventures in Enrichment

The thing about three-year-olds is that they appear normal some of the time. This lulls you into a false sense of security and causes you to make all sorts of bad judgments. Among the worst you can make is planning a big family outing for the benefit of your child.

Oh, I know it's hard. You think because now you've got a walking, talking child with a real haircut and $20 Barney sneakers that it's time to start educating him on the wider aspects of the world around him. In short, you think you might want to enrich his life with field trips and new experiences. Take my advice. Don't. Just don't. Wait until the kid is five and has become more reasonable.

Why, you ask? I can see you need a reality check. Here are some potential outings that may have already occurred to you—and some likely outcomes.

Disneyland: The Vision

The Magic Kingdom! You have many fond memories of Disneyland from when you were a small child, and you can't wait to introduce your young one to the land of enchantment! He'll marvel at the monorail and thrill to the Pirates of the Caribbean. You'll show him your favorite childhood spots, including Tom Sawyer's Island and that science ride where you turn into a molecule. Of course, you'll get him his own pair of mouse ears with his name sewed on the front (you still have yours up in the attic somewhere), and you've got the camcorder ready for his first encounter with his hero, Mickey Mouse. You look forward to the whole family roaming the park, enjoying the sights and sounds of other young families just like yours to the tune of Dixieland melodies.

Disneyland: Reality

Things have changed since you were a little kid, bucko. It now costs upward of $100 just to get in the door at this aging theme park, but first you have to crawl through bumper-to-bumper traffic along the mini-mall–lined streets of the world's most depressing suburb, Anaheim, California. Hike in from the distant outer parking lots and hope you don't get mugged, as happened to one family you read about. Hold onto your child, because the crowds are so dense you can barely see where you're going. After wandering for more than an hour, learn that they've closed Tom Sawyer's Island as a security risk, and that whole other sections of the park have been closed for repairs. Wait in line for half an hour for the Pirates of the Caribbean, then soothe your screaming child after he mistakes the mechanical pirates for the real thing. Buy a $7 hot dog and a $4 Coke to try to calm him down. Don't even try to keep him from the ubiquitous shops selling overpriced Disney merchandise. Buy the sweatshirt and the key ring, and ignore him when he asks where the Pokémon are, then call it a day and prepare for the long hike back to the car. Again, hope you don't get mugged.

The Zoo: The Vision

Your son loves bears. He has bear books, bear toys, bear pajamas. Why not take him to see the real bears? Take a Sunday and go to the zoo, the same one you used to go to as a child. Introduce him to all the animals, but watch his face when he gets to see the real live bears! The bears sunning themselves, rooting for berries, and taking care of bear cubs. A zookeeper will come by and, noticing your son's rapt attention, tell him all about taking care of the bears. After viewing all the bears, including the neat polar bears, you'll eat a nice lunch, take a ride on the zoo train, and buy him a cool bear poster for his room before heading home. He'll fall fast asleep in the car, tuckered out from his big adventure.

The Zoo: Reality

Pick a Sunday and go to the zoo. Realize that every other family on the planet also picked this particular Sunday to go to the zoo. Fight traffic. Pay for parking. Hike in from the outer lots. Pay outrageous entrance fee. Realize you schlepped the stroller for nothing when your toddler sees the zoo's "animal-o-biles" and insists you rent one of those instead. Your child complains about being hungry, about it being too hot, about being bored, even as you push him from cage to cage. When you find the bear exhibit, the bears are holed up inside their caves to hide from the heat. Explain this in vain to your whining toddler, then think of something quick to explain what the baboons in the next cage are doing to each other. Your son doesn't seem to be interested in a bear poster (which are selling for $30, anyway) but wants a wax dinosaur instead, which then melts in the car on the way home. Your son screams himself to sleep before dinner over it.

The Beach: The Vision

A perfect, sunny day at your favorite beach! You'll run along the shore with your child, showing her how to listen for the ocean in a seashell and scoop up sandcrabs with her hands.

Daddy can carry her out a little ways on his shoulders, and she'll squeal with delight as she gets splashed by a wave. Enjoy a picnic of sandwiches, hard-boiled eggs, and fruit, after which your child will content herself making sandcastles nearby while you relax with a novel. Later on, she'll nap under the umbrella, and you can all drive home with that blissed-out, salty exhaustion you get after a day well-spent at the shore.

The Beach: Reality

Wake to a perfect, sunny day, only to find it cold and overcast when you drive to the beach. If it is still perfect and sunny, you'll find the beach parking lot crowded to overflowing, and you'll have to park blocks away. Schlepp everything down to the beach and find a space on the sand. You'll have to make two trips, however, since your three-year-old will decide she can't walk on the sand because her toes will get sandy. Carry her to the blanket. Fight her tooth and claw to get the sunscreen on her, even though she then won't leave the confines of the beach umbrella. Fight her again to get her T-shirt off and her bathing suit on. It's not the right bathing suit, she'll tell you. She wanted to wear the green one you left at home. The one she said she didn't want to wear this morning. The water will terrify her, and she'll scream if you try to get her anywhere near it. Ditto sandcrabs. She won't eat the sandwiches, either. Ten minutes into your day at the beach, she'll announce that she wants to go home.

Car Trip: The Vision

Are you insane?

Car Trip: Reality
You are insane.

The Outside World

And it comes to pass that unless you're a real control freak, the outside world starts to pry its tentacles into your small child's carefully protected sphere of influence. The toddler years are the years of videos, of "Sesame Street" characters and purple dinosaurs, and of first movies. They are also the years of preschools or toddler gym classes without Mommy. Three-year-olds understand much more about what's going on around them than do their younger counterparts, and they're much more likely to mimic what they see. This is good and bad.

It's good to see your three-year-old demonstrate empathy, for example. Parents in my courtyard beam with pride when they watch their three-year-olds run up to younger children who've fallen down and pick them up, brush them off, and offer them comfort. It's a good sign when you hear them tell younger children, "Don't run in the street" or "You should share your toys." Three-year-olds love to instruct the younger set.

It's more alarming when you see your three-year-old pretending to smoke (especially when you don't smoke yourself!) or shoot you with a gun. "You're DEAD!" many boys in my courtyard thrill to say as they shoot us with their fingers or pieces of wood or a toy sword. Naturally, all of us progressive graduate-student types cringe and wonder what to say in retort.

It's always perplexing, and a bit sad, to watch a three-year-old child run into a store and announce that he wants to "buy this and this and this and this and this, too!" Our culture turns small children into good little consumers so quickly, and it somehow does it right underneath our noses.

My friend Kate told me recently that the favorite activity of her three-year-old son is poring through the toy catalogs that come in the mail. "He goes through them like they're books," she says. "And he tells himself all the things that he likes the best." I think most three-year-olds like to do this. My daughter does it, so do a lot of other three-year-olds in the courtyard. Why? Maybe they see us perusing the catalogs and want to imitate the sighs and longing looks. But where do they get the idea that they can buy all this stuff?

But you get to deal with both the heartwarming and the chilling as your older toddler examines the world around him and brings whole selections of it home with him. It goes part and parcel with growing up. Toddlers observe and imitate, and no matter how much you *tell* them what's going on, they'll draw their own conclusions based on what they *see*.

And watch out. "Toddlers have such uncluttered minds, they see *everything*," says my neighbor Misti.

My neighbor Jane and I share a love of eating out instead of cooking. Pizza, Chinese takeout, burritos—anything but having to think about making dinner after a tiring day. It's a trait our husbands share with us, thank God. But now, our three-year-olds share it, too. Just the other day, Jane tells me, when she announced that it was lunchtime, her daughter Claudia responded, "Good. Where are we going?"

Most Favored Parent Status

Heard about Daddy's little girl? She's a three-year-old.

At some point in your child's toddler tenure, he or she will decide which parent he or she likes best and make you both feel terrible in the process. I'd like to be able to say that it's usually an opposite-sex kind of thing, but that's only the case half of the time. There are little girls who won't let their daddies come near them, and little boys who act as though Mommy doesn't exist anymore now that they've been weaned. You can imagine all the insecurities this dredges up. But just when you're about to concede defeat, the toddler abruptly switches preferences, and you're back in his or her good graces, while the other of you is hung out to dry.

This is all perfectly normal, the experts assure us. It mostly has to do with a toddler exploring his feelings for the opposite sex and learning how to flirt.

For moms, this means that your girl children will actually begin to flirt, yes, flirt, with their daddies. You'll be able to glean all sorts of potential insights into their future mating patterns as you watch them engage the main men in their lives. It can be both amusing and perplexing. Where did she learn how to laugh and toss her hair like the Prell shampoo model? Who taught her how to bat her eyes and giggle like that? And why is it working so well on Daddy? Hey!

Little boys, on the other hand, become very oedipal about their mothers. It's not uncommon for a three-year-old boy to announce his intentions to marry his mother and growl at his father if he comes too close.

This can be cute, except when it's not, like when you're the unfavored parent and you get to spend the day with a glowering toddler.

When your toddler is in the grip of a strong parental preference, let's say for Daddy, it's hard to get anything done if you're the parent on the outs. Your attempts at discipline during the day are likely to be met with howls of protest and multiple declarations of "I don't like you! I want my Daddy!" You won't be able to look at her, feed her, bathe her, get her down for a nap, or even engage her in games. Try to be adult about this and not let it get to you, or your surliness will only fuel her conviction that Daddy is better.

Three-year-olds aren't fools. By this time they've discovered that not only are they independent from you, but that you two are different people as well. Mommy and Daddy have different styles when it comes to parenting. Each one has different weaknesses. Each one has a different view about, say, how many videos they'll allow before dinner. Even when your three-year-old is strongly favoring Daddy over you, that preference can switch on a dime when she wants a treat before dinner but knows Daddy won't cough up the goldfish crackers as easily as you will.

There are other factors to the favorite parent game. Not surprisingly, Mom is always the favored parent when the chips are down. Even if a toddler has spent all day ignoring you and waiting for Daddy's return, rest assured that if the scrape on the knee is ugly enough to draw blood, you're once again tops in her eyes.

Three is usually the age when children actively begin to pattern themselves after the parent of the same sex, however. So at some point, your toddler will abruptly glom onto the parent of the same sex, even if he's been ignoring that parent for months.

Diane's son Avery thrills to sit with his father and uncles and watch the football games on TV. He claps when they clap, yells when they yell. He insists on a juice box because everyone else has a beer. "He has no idea what's going on," says Diane. "But he's got to do whatever he sees his daddy doing. He's even started to pee standing up."

Little girls start realizing that there are "girl" things and "boy" things, and that boy things are blue and girl things are pink. I was shocked the first time my daughter pointed to her baby brother's socks and said, "Mommy, he can't wear those! They have flowers on them. He's a boy!" (I was also shocked she didn't demand them back because they were, after all, her old socks.) But where did she get that from? Certainly not from me. (Jackson's been wearing all of Annie's old baby clothes.) My friend Susan's three-year-old has discovered nail polish recently.

Didn't gender stereotyping of this kind go out of vogue in the '70s? Nobody in our generation actively goes out of their way to buy their girl children frilly pink dresses and cute little dollies, at least nobody in my part of the country. And yet, our three-year-old girls beg for dresses. And our boys chew their toast into gun shapes and proceed to annihilate everyone in the room.

Preschool Cool

Back in the late '60s when I went to preschool, preschool was a sweet little two- or three-hour break for Mom. We sang songs. We colored in books. We ate animal crackers and drank juice. Maybe we had a little nap. Then our moms, fresh from the hairdresser or their afternoon martinis, picked us up and took us home.

But sometime in the last ten or fifteen years, preschool got serious. Educated, upscale parents began viewing preschool as the first in many steps toward entrée to the Ivy Leagues and as such, began making preschool admission an elaborate game of one-upmanship.

There are preschools in Manhattan and San Francisco that cost upward of $10,000 a year and have waiting lists parents scramble to get on before their children are even conceived. There are complicated applications, complete with mandatory letters of recommendation and entrance interviews for you and the child. Parents coach their children in what to say and how to act, and consider it a disappointing blow if their child doesn't make the cut.

We in the provinces used to laugh at such foolery. Now, however, with the economy gone nova, more and more people are starting to play this preschool game. These days you can hardly celebrate your child's three-year birthday without dozens of people asking what preschool you're enrolling him in.

There are as many different kinds of preschools to choose from as there are flavors of ice cream. There are Montessori schools, based on educational ideas developed in Rome in 1907. There are bilingual schools, French-American schools, Jewish preschools, Muslim preschools, and Christian preschools. There are preschools that emphasize academics and preschools that emphasize play. Hundreds of books and thousands of articles have been written to guide you on how best to choose a preschool for your particular child. And you thought you wouldn't have to deal with this kind of thing until college.

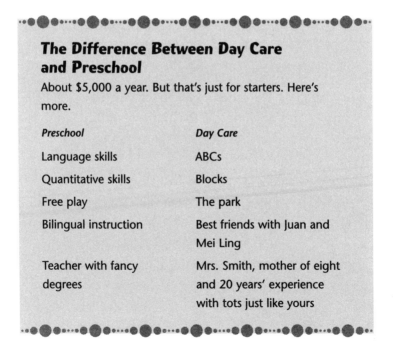

The Difference Between Day Care and Preschool

About $5,000 a year. But that's just for starters. Here's more.

Preschool	Day Care
Language skills	ABCs
Quantitative skills	Blocks
Free play	The park
Bilingual instruction	Best friends with Juan and Mei Ling
Teacher with fancy degrees	Mrs. Smith, mother of eight and 20 years' experience with tots just like yours

What's a three-year-old supposed to be learning, anyway? Most experts agree that children this age learn best through play, and that free play in a stimulating environment is better than any kind of structured classroom experience. They agree that they learn best through peer interaction rather than through adult-led instruction. By these guidelines, all three-year-olds should be allowed to make mudpies in the park with a handful of other young children.

But try telling that to the great hordes who are bent on enriching the minds of their progeny. If the Joneses down the street are sending their three-year-old to preschool, then surely you'd better rush to do the same.

Imagination Overload

My brain hurts just trying to keep up with the imagination of my daughter. The other morning she created a cash register out of the treading on the bottom of her boot. She plugged in the boot laces on either side of her leg, then looked at me seriously.

"What would you like to order today?"

Three-year-olds are rarely what they appear to be. More likely they're mermaids. Or rampaging elephants. Or baby puppies. Sometimes, they're you. Sometimes, they're whomever their best friend of the moment is at day care. If you come across a three-year-old who is not engaged in deep fantasy play, then chances are it's a three-year-old who is engaged in deep slumber.

Why is this? It's the charming result of a year and a half of imagination buildup. Imagination kicks in for babies at around eighteen months and grows steadily, blooming, I like to think, at three, before socialization tempers it at four. A three-year-old is aware of everything that's going on around her and now has the brain power to ask about it, process it, and incorporate it into play. And perhaps you've already noticed, toddlers play from the very moment they wake up in the morning until they pass out at night.

You have to factor imagination into your every dealing with older toddlers. It can be your friend or it can be your enemy, depending on how well you know your child and how much imagination you still possess.

Take the monster problem, for example. Three-year-olds have started to clue into things that scare them in books, videos, and their own heads. Suddenly, they can see strange shapes in the shadows of their own rooms at night. Our own readings of fairy tales and stories they hear from their friends reinforce the realization that there are scary things out there, and that they should be frightened. Of what, they're not sure. But they have a name for this chilling unknown: monsters.

Monsters have to be dealt with every night. They're as ubiquitous as the stuffed animal collections in the rooms of older toddlers. As a parent, you can reassure them that there are no such things as monsters and there are certainly none in their room, although this won't get you very far. A much better way to handle monsters is to tap in to your inner toddler and forge a solution from that perspective.

My friend Dana bought a cheap spray bottle and filled it with water and blue food coloring. This, she informed her three-year-old son, is Monster Spray. Every night after the story, she'd spray his room for monsters, taking care not to miss the dark corners or the closet or behind the shades. It worked every time.

I've told my daughter that monsters are too afraid of me to venture into her room.

"And you know what happens when I get mad, don't you?"

She blinks up at me, her blankets pulled up to her chin. "You'll yell at them?"

"Worse than that," I say. "If any monsters dare come into your room, I'LL EAT THEM! HA HA!"

To date I've only had to consume a small handful of monsters. (They taste just like chicken.)

If you can't get down with your own imagination, you're in for lots more hassle in your everyday dealings with the toddler of the house. Friends of mine, Debbie and Scott, illustrate this well. Debbie is very literal-minded (that's why she's an accountant), while her husband, Scott, is not. Debbie takes her three-year-old son Tyler's every request very seriously and tries to resolve his need of the moment. As anyone in the Toddler Summit could tell her, this can only lead to madness. Tyler will be pretending to cook and will ask his mommy to give him the salt, pepper, and "other spices." Debbie will hand him the actual salt container but lecture him first on how not to spill it all over the kitchen floor. Then she'll warn him about the pepper and tell him not to get any into his eyes. Finally, she'll ask for a complete list of spices he has in mind so that she can determine whether or not they're child-appropriate.

Scott, on the other hand, just whips the magic invisible salt shaker out of his pocket when Tyler asks and pours some over whatever he's "cooking." Ditto the pepper. The "spices" come from imaginary containers in the bottom drawer. Tyler is happy as a sand boy that Daddy is helping him cook and thrilled that Dad so easily joins him in the fantasy. He never wanted the actual items at all.

This lesson can extend to almost everything a three-year-old tells you she wants over the course of the day. In fact, you should just routinely offer her imaginary objects before you try the real thing, just to see if she's playing (news flash: she usually is!). You'll cut down on the number of random things you'll be begged to procure.

Around this time is when imaginary friends make an appearance as well. Blame imagination for spilled juice, Play-Doh in the carpet, artwork on the walls, and poop accidents in the afternoon. Most three-year-olds clue in to the handy concept of *blame*, and believe they're putting one over us when they can blame someone else for these sorts of gaffes. So much the better if we can't actually see this playmate, right?

When dealing with an imaginary playmate, it's best to be nonchalant about it. If you make too big a deal, your toddler might end up irritated with you for trying to co-opt his friend. Or he may up and chastise you, "Daddy, Bobo's not a *real* dinosaur! He's just *pretend*!" And then won't you feel stupid? Better to simply include Bobo in family functions as if he were a normal friend, and don't object if your toddler declines to let him stay for dinner.

When the imaginary friend gets the blame for havoc wreaked about the house, just ask your toddler to ask Bobo to be more careful next time. Sometimes, your tot will try to get an extra dish of ice cream for this imaginary friend (wouldn't you?). Simply say that Bobo (or whomever) has told you that he doesn't like pink ice cream. And leave it at that. He'll insist. Just say no.

Your three-year-old is probably the most imaginative creature you'll ever meet. Go out of your way to encourage this. Let him or her dress up in your old stuff. Let them play with harmless kitchen utensils and spend too long in the bathtub. Let them play all day in the autumn leaves if they want to, and permit them to start a leaf collection, even if it means you have to pick up crumbling leaf bits for the next two weeks. Revel in their imagination, and you'll never be bored.

At the same time, never tease him about his fantasies. Three-year-olds are serious about their imaginative games, and you do them a disservice by laughing at or dismissing them. These fantasies are actually very important work. They're the way he makes sense of the world around him, and they will never again be so complete or so innocent. Let him play. By four he'll start tempering these fantasies himself as he comes into more contact with his peers, and this magical year will be lost to memory and an overstuffed photo album. I guarantee you you'll miss it.

EPILOGUE

It was the best of times; it was the worst of times. But you did it. The Attack of the Toddlers has washed over you, and you've emerged out the other end a stronger, more patient parent. No phase of childhood (with the notable exception of adolescence) drags you through the extremes of emotion quite like toddlerhood. Just when you think you're going to lose it, the little tyke melts your heart. How do they do it? It's a great parental mystery.

Worst of Times

You're run ragged from juggling work and family life with a toddler.

Best of Times
You're greeted by delighted screams and a full-body hug when you arrive to pick up that toddler at the end of the day.

Worst of Times
Your toddler throws himself violently on the floor of the A&P when you tell him he doesn't need Cheese Doodles today. Everybody glowers at you.

Best of Times
The next day, the same toddler launches into a rousing—and very creative—rendition of the ABCs. Everybody smiles and remarks on what a prodigy you have.

Worst of Times
Your home is a shadow of its former self.

Best of Times
You remember that Martha Stewart had toddlers long before she was rich and famous.

Worst of Times
She fights you every step of the way on her first trip to the zoo.

Best of Times
Once there, she is awestruck. She learns all the animal sounds in an afternoon and decides later that night that baths are fun because she's a hippo.

Worst of Times
You catch every new strain of stomach flu that comes into town.

Best of Times
As you lay on the couch, your two-and-a-half-year-old plays quietly nearby, periodically coming over to stroke your head and feed you grapes.

Worst of Times
She acts like she's being killed when you try to wash her hair at bathtime.

Best of Times
You prefer the smell of her after she's bathed, jammied, and nestled in your arms to your $75-an-ounce eau de cologne any day.

Worst of Times
You've nearly given yourself a coronary chasing him around the park, keeping him away from the ducks in the pond, and preventing ownership battles in the sandbox.

Best of Times
He falls asleep in the stroller on the way home, and everyone comments on your angelic child as you drink a coffee in peace and quiet.

Best of Times
After three years of battle, your toddler utters a conciliatory sentence or commits a selfless deed, indicating that the Attack of the Toddlers may be at an end.

READINGS FOR THEM (AND YOU)

I know. Since you're sitting here reading this book, I'm preaching to the converted when I tell you how important it is to read to your child. But since we've got more bookcases than matching dishes at my house, allow me to make a few book suggestions that will drive your toddler wild with happiness. They will, alas, also drive you to distraction, since you'll be commanded to read them again and again and again and again.

One Year to Eighteen Months

Very simple books with lots of interactive potential. Because babies this age like to point and wiggle.

Brown Bear, Brown Bear, What Do You See? Bill Martin, Jr. (New York: Henry Holt, 1996). Great big animals in big, bright colors.

Count! Denise Fleming (New York: Henry Holt, 1992). Teach your tot to count to ten while teaching him how to wiggle, jump, stretch, and hop, too.

Time for Bed, Mem Fox (New York: Harcourt Brace, 1997). Sweet and simple bedtime rhymes show animals and their babies.

Two to Three Years

These guys like repetition and whimsy, although it's hard to say which they like more. They also like details they can hunt out while you're still looking.

Going on a Bear Hunt, Michael Rosen and Helen Oxenbury (London: Walker Books, 1989). This family is never going on a bear hunt again, but you'll be reading this book to your toddler twice a night for months.

Good Night, Gorilla, Peggy Rathmann (New York: Putnam, 1996). A cardboard book with no words but a bright pictorial story with lots of repeating details. Find the red balloon in every one.

Hop on Pop, Dr. Seuss (New York: Random House, 1963) and *The Foot Book*, Dr. Seuss (New York: Random House, 1968). You can't go wrong with Dr. Seuss, especially the "Bright and Early Books for Beginning Readers" series. Toddlers love the weird illustrations and wacky rhymes almost as much as you love reading them. Remember them from your day?

Three Years and Beyond

Preschoolers like stories they can follow as much as colorful pictures.

Choo Choo: The Story of the Little Engine Who Ran Away, Virginia Lee Burton (New York: Houghton Mifflin, 1937). Before Thomas the Tank Engine, there was Choo Choo. A classic with good reason.

Everybody Poops, Taro Gomi (New York: Kane/Miller Book Publishers, 1993). The perfect three-year-old book that focuses on a favorite three-year-old topic.

Ten Minutes to Bedtime, Peggy Rathmann (New York: Putnam, 1998). Another brilliant book by the illustrator behind *Goodnight, Gorilla*. This one involves a Hamster Bedtime Tour, with dozens of repeating details your toddler will thrill to find.

The Tiger Who Came to Tea, Judith Kerr (London: William Collins, 1968). A whimsical tale involving a tiger who comes to tea and eats everything in the house.

Videos

I'm an unabashed anti-TV snob, but I'm still the first to admit that a toddler can get a lot of learning and fun out of a quality video. Here are a few of my favorites:

Disney. Stick to the classics, and you can't go wrong. *Dumbo, Lady and the Tramp, Pinocchio,* and *Snow White* are all good choices for toddlers. The earlier movies have a slower, more innocent quality that the newer animated features lack.

Richard Scarey. The famous cartoonist with the strange name also makes great toddler viewing. Sweet and simple, with catchy music, his ABCs and counting videos are some of the best.

Sesame Street. You can't go wrong with most of the original *Sesame Street* videos. The best wrap vintage *Sesame Street* skits around a central theme such as learning how to share, singing the alphabet, or counting to ten. *The Best of Elmo* and *Elmo's World* are particularly sure to please the toddler set. Avoid the more commercial compilations such as *Elmopalooza,* which focus too much on celebrity culture.

Readings for You

Don't understand your toddler? These professionals can help.

The Language Instinct, Steven Pinker (Harper Perennial, 1994). An engrossing book that just also happens to have a brilliant chapter on how babies and toddlers acquire their language skills. This chapter alone is worth the price of the book.

The Magic Years, Selma H. Fraiberg (Charles Scribner's Sons, 1959). Another classic that helps you get under the hood of your toddler. She aptly likens toddlers to magicians and goes from there.

Toddlers and Preschoolers, Lawrence Kutner (Avon, 1994). A handy and readable little book that touches on all things toddler.

Touchpoints: Your Child's Emotional and Behavioral Development, T. Berry Brazelton (Addison-Wesley, 1992). The good doctor explains just what's going on in the heads of our children and reassures us that, no, we're not nuts—and neither are our toddlers.